THE BIBLE STORY

VOLUME V

---·•·---

GREAT MEN OF GOD

(From Elijah to the Fall of Jerusalem)

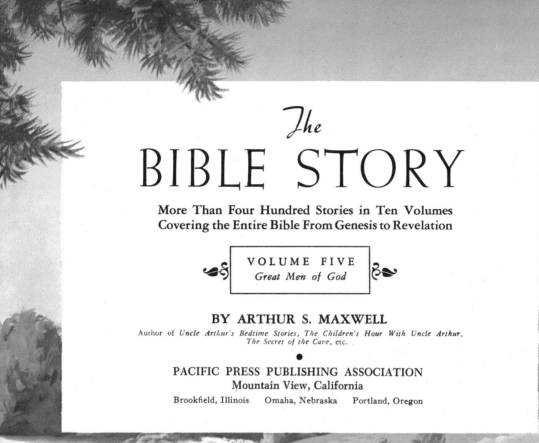

The
BIBLE STORY

More Than Four Hundred Stories in Ten Volumes
Covering the Entire Bible From Genesis to Revelation

VOLUME FIVE
Great Men of God

BY ARTHUR S. MAXWELL

Author of *Uncle Arthur's Bedtime Stories, The Children's Hour With Uncle Arthur,*
The Secret of the Cave, etc.

●

PACIFIC PRESS PUBLISHING ASSOCIATION
Mountain View, California

Brookfield, Illinois   Omaha, Nebraska   Portland, Oregon

CONTENTS

5

← PAINTING BY RUSSELL HARLAN   © 1955, BY REVIEW AND HERALD

Under wise teachers in the synagogue schools
boys and girls of the Jewish nation received
moral instruction and training in useful arts
that would make them leaders of their people.

Part III—Stories of Conflict and Blessing

Part IV—Stories of Kings and Prophets

PART I

Stories of Elijah

(1 KINGS 17:1-2 KINGS 2:15)

STORY 1

Boy With a Wonderful Name

NOT long after King Solomon died, a little boy was born in the land of Gilead, east of the river Jordan. The Bible does not tell us anything about his parents, not even their names. But they must have been very good people, because they called their precious little son Elijah, which means "My God is Jehovah."

What a wonderful name for a boy!

No doubt his parents dedicated him to God from his birth, and prayed that he would grow up to be a brave and noble champion of truth and right.

From time to time, in their little home far from Jerusalem, they heard about the dreadful things going on in the holy city—how the idols that Solomon's wives had set up were now being worshiped all over the place—and they made up their minds that whatever happened they would remain true to Jehovah, the God of Abraham, Isaac, Jacob—and David.

9

In the midst of the idolatry and wickedness of Israel the parents of Elijah taught him to worship the true God, and God called him to be one of the great prophets to His people.

By and by news reached them that Jeroboam, the new king of Israel, had even made golden calves and told the people that these were the gods that brought them out of Egypt!

Thus Elijah grew up at a time when people were taking sides between the God of heaven and the gods of the heathen. As he talked with other boys he knew, some of them would say, "We worship Baal; he's the best god"; and others, "We like Ashtoreth better; you should just see what goes on in front of that idol"; and still others, "We go to Moloch's temple; things are much more exciting there." And then Elijah would say, very bravely, "But my God is Jehovah."

Nothing could move him from this stand. No matter how much the other boys and girls jeered at him, he would answer them fearlessly, "My God is Jehovah."

The more he saw of the evil that was done in connection with the worship of idols, the more sure he was that he was right. How could the people be so blind, so stupid, he wondered, as to think that God was pleased with all this wickedness? How could they believe that He wanted little children burned as sacrifices, as was done in the temple of Moloch? It was all so wrong, so very wrong, that it made him resolve to give himself, his life, his all, to teaching the people about the true God.

Talking with other boys and girls, mixing with the people in village market places, or alone on the mountainside, he would tell himself again and again, "My God is Jehovah," "My God is Jehovah."

BOY WITH A WONDERFUL NAME

So his name became part of himself. And people came to know him as the strange lad who hated idols and worshiped the God of heaven. They said he was old-fashioned and out of date. They told him he wouldn't get anywhere in life if he held on to such foolish notions. But God's eye was upon him. Here was a boy He could use. Here was the champion He was looking for!

And what a destiny was his!

Today, nearly three thousand years later, the eyes of the Lord still run "to and fro throughout the whole earth, to shew himself strong in the behalf of them whose heart is perfect toward him." Everywhere His ears are listening eagerly for those precious words of loyalty, "My God is Jehovah!" Blessed are the boys and girls who utter them from love-filled hearts. What a destiny lies before *them!* How much God will do for them, here and hereafter!

You too can be a boy—or a girl—with a wonderful name. Just make the same decision as did Elijah. Say, "My God is Jehovah," just now—and mean it.

STORY 2

God's Messenger

FAR from the cities of Judah and Israel, out in the rugged, unsettled region of Gilead, Elijah grew to manhood. Like John the Baptist, who lived in the same place years afterward, he knew nothing of life's comforts. Food was scarce. Clothes were hard to get. His only luxury was talking with God.

Many times he must have wondered why God did not do something about all the wickedness in the land. Many times he must have looked up into the skies and cried, "How long, O Lord, how long?"

Then at last God spoke—as He always does when His time has come. He told Elijah to go to Ahab, now king of Israel, and tell him that because of his sins a great drought would come upon the country; that there would be neither dew nor rain for years.

It was not a pleasant message to take to a king, but fearlessly Elijah set out to deliver it. Without a thought of danger to himself, he made his way over the mountain trails to Samaria, where Ahab had set up his new capital and built a temple to Baal.

Arriving in the city, he walked up the busy main street that led to the palace on the hill. Passing the guards at the gate, he entered the hall where the king was sitting on his throne, with many courtiers around him.

Quickly all eyes turned to the stranger who had suddenly appeared in their midst. Who was this man dressed in a rough garment of haircloth and a girdle of leather? What was he doing in the king's court?

Soon the prophet's voice, strong and powerful, rang upon the ears of the assembly.

"As the Lord God of Israel liveth, before whom I stand, there shall not be dew nor rain these years, but according to my word."

What happened next we are not told. But there must have been quite a stir.

"Is the man mad?" Ahab may well have said. "Does he think he can control the dew and the rain? Does he think his god is stronger than Baal?" At this the courtiers laughed, jeering at Elijah as he made his way to the door and disappeared.

But Elijah's warning was no laughing matter. The dry weather began, just as he said it would. Day after day the sun beat down upon the parched land out of a cloudless sky. There was no dew by night, nor rain by day. Soon the whole countryside took on a deep-brown hue. Not a green blade of grass was to be seen anywhere. Cattle roamed far and wide looking for something to eat. Streams ran dry. The water level in wells dropped alarmingly.

Winter came and passed, and still there was no rain. People watched the clouds in vain. They passed over and left no moisture.

Spring arrived. The land was almost too hard to plow. Farmers sowed seed they had saved from the small crop of the year before, but it hardly began to grow before it shriveled up.

Now cattle began to die by hundreds. The bodies of bony cows, sheep, and goats lay unburied for the crows and buzzards to eat.

Everybody was worried now, from the king in his palace to the humblest shepherd on the hills. All knew that they were facing starvation and ruin. But instead of praying to God they turned to Baal, Ashtoreth, and Moloch. "Send us rain!" they cried to their idols, but no rain came.

Another blazing summer passed, another scorching autumn, another winter of rainless clouds passing overhead.

GOD'S MESSENGER

Would there never be an end to this dreadful drought? people wondered. Must Palestine turn into a desert?

Many times King Ahab thought about the man who had come to see him in his palace—the man who had claimed to be a prophet of Jehovah and said there would be no dew or rain unless he said so. Perhaps he *did* know how to control the weather. Perhaps he was able to keep rain from falling on the earth. Where was he? He must be found at all costs. He must be made to break the spell he had put on the country.

So a price was put on Elijah's head. Orders went out that he was to be brought to Samaria at once. But nobody could find him. He had disappeared.

Growing more and more desperate, the king sent messengers to Egypt, to Syria, to Mesopotamia, seeking Elijah. There was, in fact, "no nation or kingdom" where they did not go in search of him.

As the messengers returned they all told the same story. They had failed in their mission. There was no trace of Elijah anywhere. Nobody had seen him or heard of him.

"Where can the man be?" fumed Ahab. "He must be somewhere. Find him!"

But they couldn't find him.

Yet he wasn't far away. Not very far. And God knew where he was all the time.

STORY 3

Fed by Ravens

WHEN Elijah left Ahab's palace, God said to him, "Get thee hence, and turn thee eastward, and hide thyself by the brook Cherith, that is before Jordan. And it shall be, that thou shalt drink of the brook; and I have commanded the ravens to feed thee there."

He knew the brook Cherith very well. No doubt as a boy he had played on its banks. As for the ravens, he remembered them too, and where they nested.

It was a long, tiresome journey, back across the Jordan and up one of the wild canyons over the mountains beyond, at the bottom of which ran the tiny stream.

Coming at last to a cave, or an overhanging rock, he stopped to rest, certain that Ahab could never find him here.

It was a lonesome, desolate spot.

Not a sound broke the silence save the distant cawing of the ravens and the tinkling of the stream as it cascaded over rocks and pebbles toward the Jordan.

16

There was no trace of man or woman, boy or girl. He was alone, utterly alone, with God.

Growing hungry, he wondered where he could find food. But there was no food anywhere, and he dared not betray his hiding place by going in search of some. The hours slipped by. Evening came. Then, just when it seemed as though he must go to sleep without a bite to eat, a raven flew overhead and dropped something. Elijah picked it up. It was food. How thankful he was!

Strange that a raven should act like this! Perhaps it was just an accident. But no; it could not be, for here came another, and another, each dropping some choice morsel that, normally, it would itself have eaten.

As Elijah looked up and saw the food falling as it were from heaven, he remembered God's promise to command the ravens to feed him. His heart overflowed with thankfulness. "My God is Jehovah," he may well have said. "Wonderful, wonderful God!"

In the morning the same thing happened. As the sun rose above the canyon walls the ravens came flying in low again, dropping their little offerings of food to this man who was a friend of God.

"And the ravens brought him bread and flesh in the morning, and bread and flesh in the evening; and he drank of the brook."

Day after day this wonderful thing happened, and Elijah marveled more and more at the goodness of God in looking after him so faithfully.

Much of the time he spent down by the brook, where the cool water helped him bear the terrible heat. Gradually he noticed the stream getting smaller and smaller, shallower and shallower. Some nights he could scarcely hear its tinkle any more. He knew then that he would soon have to leave this hiding place and find another. But where could he go? Where would he be safe from the anger of Ahab? But he had no need to worry. God was thinking of him and planning for him.

Finally, when the last little trickle of water had disappeared and the last little pool in the bed of the

18

brook had dried up, God said to him, "Get thee to Zarephath, which belongeth to Zidon, and dwell there: behold, I have commanded a widow woman there to sustain thee."

Elijah understood at once. God was sending him far north of Samaria to a little city near the coast.

Bidding his friends the ravens farewell, and gathering up their last little gifts of love—for he knew he would find no food on his journey—he set out for Zarephath.

Day after day he trudged on, over rocky hillsides and steep mountain trails. How tired he must have been! How hungry! How very, very thirsty!

Weary, hot, and dusty, he drew near at last to Zarephath. Now he could see the outline of the city wall; now the gate he would have to enter. How glad he was that his long, tiresome journey was almost over! But how would he find the woman who was to care for him?

God had not told him her name, or where she lived. Was she rich or poor, old or young? All he knew about her was that she was a widow—and there must be many widows in Zarephath. How would he know the right one? With Ahab's soldiers looking for him everywhere, he must not make a mistake.

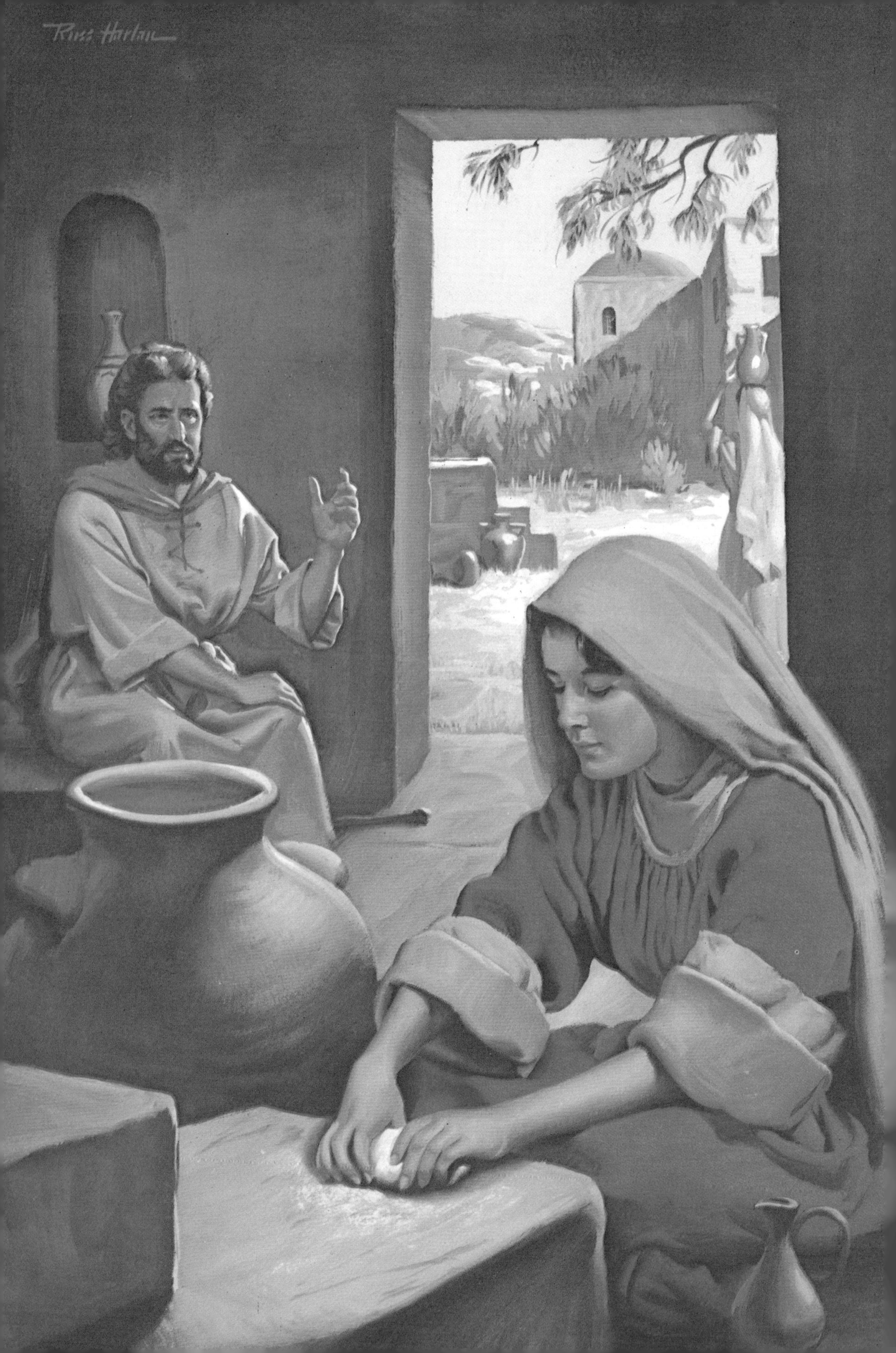
Russ Harlan

STORY 4

The Never-Empty Barrel

A S ELIJAH was wondering what to do next, he saw a woman gathering sticks not far from the city gate.

"Water!" he called to her. "Fetch me, I pray thee, a little water in a vessel, that I may drink."

Looking up, the woman felt sorry for the poor stranger, and hurried off to get some water for him. As she did so she heard him calling to her again.

"Bring me something to eat, too," he said.

The woman stopped, and a great sadness came over her.

"As the Lord thy God liveth," she said, "I have not a cake, but an handful of meal in a barrel, and a little oil in a cruse: and, behold, I am gathering two sticks, that I may go in and dress it for me and my son, that we may eat it, and die."

Elijah could see she was telling him the truth, and he was sorry for her. He felt sure now that this must be the widow whom God had commanded to sustain him, a widow so poor

21

During the time of terrible famine in Israel a poor widow shared her last loaf of bread with the prophet Elijah and God honored her faith by keeping her jars full of oil and meal.

she had nothing in the world except a handful of meal and a little oil. In such case he knew something wonderful was bound to happen, and soon.

"Fear not," he said kindly to the poor widow; "go and do as thou hast said: but make me thereof a little cake first, and bring it unto me, and after make for thee and for thy son. For thus saith the Lord God of Israel, The barrel of meal shall not waste, neither shall the cruse of oil fail, until the day that the Lord sendeth rain upon the earth."

It may have sounded selfish for him to say, "Make me a cake first," but it really wasn't, for Elijah's faith in God was so great that to him the barrel of meal was already full and the cruse of oil overflowing. He was absolutely sure that if the poor widow trusted God's promise enough to make him a little cake *first,* then God would never cease to bless her in many wonderful ways.

The widow decided to trust God. She took Him at His word. Going to her house, she looked in the meal barrel. Just as she had told Elijah, there was only a handful of meal at the bottom of it. She scraped it out into a little pile. Then she went to the oil jug. Tipping it up, she drained out the last drop, or so she thought.

After mixing the oil and meal into a paste, she prepared to light the fire. Just then, maybe, her son came running in. I can hear him saying, "Is that cake for me, Mamma?"

"No, darling, it's for the man of God who has come to see us."

"But I'm hungry."

THE NEVER-EMPTY BARREL

"I know, dear, but he has promised me that God won't let us starve."

The fire blazed up. The little cake was put on the hot bricks. It began to brown, and soon filled the lowly kitchen with a sweet aroma.

Suddenly there was an excited cry from the boy. "Mamma, I thought you said there was no more meal in the barrel; but there is!"

"No, darling, there can't be. I scraped the last of it out just now."

"But there is, there is! See, Mamma! It's nice, new meal, too!"

The poor widow looked in the barrel and could hardly believe her eyes. There *was* meal there! More than there had been for many days. She turned to the cruse of oil and tipped it up. Oil flowed out. It was too wonderful! Joy filled her heart. She looked over at Elijah, sitting there waiting for his

little cake. There was a beautiful smile on his tired face, a smile of sheer delight that God had honored his faith so soon.

Not only Elijah ate that night, but the widow and her son. They had not enjoyed so good a meal in many days.

And because the widow did "according to the saying of Elijah," it turned out that "she, and he, and her house, did eat many days. And the barrel of meal wasted not, neither did the cruse of oil fail, according to the word of the Lord, which he spake by Elijah."

What a wonderful time the angels must have had putting meal in that barrel and filling up that cruse of oil! How happy they must have been watching the surprise on the widow's face when she discovered what had happened!

But this was not the only blessing God sent to reward her for her kindness to His servant.

One day her son became very ill. Lovingly she tended him, but he became worse and worse. Feeling sure he was dying, she took him in her arms, and there he breathed his last breath.

"Elijah! Elijah!" she cried. The man of God came down from the loft, where he was living. He saw at once what had happened.

"Give me thy son," he said to the widow, taking the limp body from the sobbing mother.

Then he climbed up into the loft again and laid the boy on his bed. "And he stretched himself upon the child three times, and cried unto the Lord, and said, O Lord my God, I pray thee, let this child's soul [breath] come into him again.

24

"And the Lord heard the voice of Elijah; and the soul [breath] of the child came into him again, and he revived."

Dumb with grief, the poor widow scarcely noticed Elijah as he clambered down from the loft again with the boy in his arms.

Then she heard the prophet speak to her. What was that he was saying?

"See, thy son liveth."

"What? Impossible!"

She rushed across the room.

It was true, true! He was alive! He was breathing again! Oh, joy! Tears of happiness and gratitude streamed down her cheeks as she cried, "By this I know that thou art a man of God, and that the word of the Lord in thy mouth is truth."

25

STORY 5

Fire From Heaven

THREE years had passed since Elijah stood in Ahab's court and announced the coming of the great drought. Part of this time he had spent by the brook Cherith, part with the widow of Zarephath.

Many times during these lonely days he must have wondered what God was planning to do next for His people. Had they learned their lesson yet? Were they ready to turn from their idols? Someday the drought must end, but how and when?

At last the word of the Lord came to him, saying, "Go, shew thyself unto Ahab; and I will send rain upon the earth."

Elijah set out at once for Samaria, a hundred and fifty miles or so to the south of Zarephath. On the way he ran into Obadiah, the governor of Ahab's house, who was searching for pasture for the horses and mules that were still alive. This good man was one of the few leaders who remained loyal to the God of heaven. He had shown his loyalty by hiding a hundred of God's prophets in a cave when Jezebel had tried to kill them. Recognizing Elijah, he dropped to his knees and cried, "Art thou that my lord Elijah?"

"I am," replied Elijah. "Go, tell thy lord, Behold, Elijah is here."

"I can't," said Obadiah. He was afraid. Ahab, he said, had been searching everywhere for Elijah. There had been many false reports as to where he had been seen, and these had served but to make the king more and more angry. "Now," said Obadiah, "if I tell Ahab you are here, and he finds you have disappeared again, he will kill me."

"As the Lord of hosts liveth, before whom I stand," said Elijah, "I will surely shew myself unto him to day."

Obadiah believed him, and rode off to find the king. On hearing the news, Ahab went at once to the place where his servant had said he would find Elijah. The prophet was still there.

"Art thou he that troubleth Israel?" he demanded angrily as he drew up his horse close to Elijah.

"I have not troubled Israel," replied Elijah without flinching; "but thou, and thy father's house, in that ye have forsaken the commandments of the Lord, and thou hast followed Baalim."

Something in the tone of the prophet's voice, or in what he said, made a deep impression on the king. He was speechless.

If he talked about the terrible drought, or the need of rain, the Bible does not say. But Elijah certainly told him what he must do if he wanted to know the blessing of God again.

"Now therefore send, and gather to me all Israel unto Mount Carmel, and the prophets of Baal four hundred and fifty, and the prophets of the groves four hundred, which eat at Jezebel's table."

No doubt Elijah explained why he wanted such a meeting—so that the people might decide once and for all whether they were going to serve the God of heaven or the false gods, whose idols had been set up all over the land.

The king agreed to the plan, perhaps as the only hope of getting rain and breaking the dreadful drought. When he returned to his palace he sent out messengers calling the people to assemble at Mount Carmel.

Soon thousands of men, women, and children were streaming toward the place of meeting. None were quite sure why they were going there, only that the king had told them to. There was a rumor that Elijah was going to be there, but nobody believed it. Similar tales had been told about the prophet for the past three years, and he had never shown up.

28

FIRE FROM HEAVEN

Hadn't the king himself been looking for him all this time?

Pushing and jostling one another, the people trudged and stumbled up toward the top of Mount Carmel until all the slopes were covered. All night long they stayed there, waiting for the dawn.

Early in the morning somebody cried, "There he is! I can see him! Elijah is here!"

Instantly the word swept through the waiting throng. Men and women strained their necks to see the man who had dared to defy the king, while boys and girls shoved their way to the front to get a better view.

"Hush!" cried someone. "Hush! He's speaking. Elijah is speaking."

Silence fell upon the milling crowd. Then from the top of the mountain came that deep, powerful voice once heard in Ahab's court.

"How long halt ye between two opinions?" cried the prophet. "If the Lord be God, follow him: but if Baal, then follow him."

Nobody spoke. "The people answered him not a word."

Elijah continued, "I, even I only, remain a prophet of the Lord; but Baal's prophets are four hundred and fifty men.

Let them therefore give us two bullocks; and let them choose one bullock for themselves, and cut it in pieces, and lay it on wood, and put no fire under: and I will dress the other bullock, and lay it on wood, and put no fire under: and call ye on the name of your gods, and I will call on the name of the Lord: and the God that answereth by fire, let him be God."

"Well said; that's fair enough," cried the people, thrilled to learn that they were to see such a test of the powers of rival gods. From now on they watched and listened with tenfold interest.

Turning to the prophets of Baal, Elijah said to them, "Choose you one bullock for yourselves, and dress it first; for ye are many; and call on the name of your gods, but put no fire under."

Glad for the chance to prove that Baal was the greatest god on earth, his prophets seized their bullock, cut it up, and placed the pieces in order on the altar they had built.

Then they began to implore their god to send fire to burn the sacrifice.

"O Baal, hear us!" they cried.

But "there was no voice, nor any that answered."

They started to leap up and down around the altar, crying, "O Baal, hear us!" but still no fire came.

All morning long they kept up the wild dancing and shouting. At noon "Elijah mocked them, and said, Cry aloud: for he is a god; either he is talking, or he is pursuing, or he is in a journey, or peradventure he sleepeth, and must be awaked."

At this they cried still louder and began to cut themselves with knives "till the blood gushed out upon them."

It did no good. Midday passed. Afternoon came. The sun began to sink toward the gray-green sea. Still "there was neither voice, nor any to answer, nor any that regarded."

Presently Elijah spoke again to the people, who were tired and disappointed in the failure of the prophets of Baal.

"Come near unto me," he cried, and the crowd surged forward.

Then they watched him repair the altar of the Lord that used to stand upon this mountaintop but had been forgotten and had broken down. Taking twelve stones, one for each of the twelve tribes of Israel, he rebuilt the altar, then dug a trench around it.

Next he "put the wood in order, and cut the bullock in pieces, and laid him on the wood."

Then, to everybody's surprise, he said, "Fill four barrels with water, and pour it on the burnt sacrifice, and on the wood."

The water was brought—maybe from the sea, for the springs had all dried up—and poured upon the altar.

31

Some said, "Does he expect it to burn, with all that water on it?" But if Elijah heard, he took no notice.

"Do it the second time," he said, and they did.

"Do it the third time," he said, and the sacrifice was soaked again until water poured into the trench and filled it. Now nobody could say he set fire to the sacrifice himself.

Suddenly a hush fell over the great assembly as Elijah raised his voice in prayer. Everybody listened, even the prophets of Baal, who had ceased their shouting.

"Lord God of Abraham, Isaac, and of Israel," he cried aloud, "let it be known this day that thou art God in Israel,

and that I am thy servant, and that I have done all these things at thy word. Hear me, O Lord, hear me, that this people may know that thou art the Lord God, and that thou hast turned their heart back again."

Scarcely had he finished praying when there was a flash of flame from the skies as "the fire of the Lord fell, and consumed the burnt sacrifice, and the wood, and the stones, and the dust, and licked up the water that was in the trench."

It was a marvelous, never-to-be-forgotten sight.

Terrified, the people fell on their faces, crying, "The Lord, he is the God; the Lord, he is the God!"

They saw what a mistake they had made in worshiping the worthless idols of Baal. From now on they would serve Jehovah, the God of Elijah. With their own eyes they had seen His power. Never again would they forget Him.

STORY 6

A Cloud Like a Man's Hand

SEEING the people on their knees before God, Elijah gave orders that the prophets of Baal, who had led them into so much wickedness, should be seized and put to death. Nobody lifted a hand to save them. Quickly he led them down to the brook Kishon and killed them all.

Then he turned to King Ahab, who had watched everything that had happened that day, and said, "Get thee up, eat and drink; for there is a sound of abundance of rain."

Ahab was glad for the chance to eat, but Elijah climbed up to the summit of Carmel again and "cast himself down upon the earth, and put his face between his knees."

There was nobody on the mountaintop now except the prophet and his servant. The crowds had gone, leaving a great stillness and loneliness.

Bowing low before God, Elijah poured forth his thanks for this day of victory—for the swift answer to his prayer, for the flash of fire from heaven, for the defeat of the prophets

35

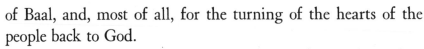

of Baal, and, most of all, for the turning of the hearts of the
people back to God.

What a wonderful day it had been, like to that when
the Red Sea opened, or when the Jordan dried up before Israel!
Not for many, many years had God revealed His power so
gloriously.

But now, thought Elijah, it was time for the rain to come.
The people were sorry for their sins. They had turned against
Baal and had helped to get rid of all his false prophets. Now
God could bless them again, if He would.

"O God!" cried Elijah, "send the rain."

He knew it would come. He was as sure of the rain as
he had been of the fire. Had he not already told Ahab that
he had heard the sound of it? Yet he prayed.

Raising his head, he said to his servant, "Go up now,
look toward the sea."

The servant obeyed, but soon returned, saying, "There
is nothing."

Again Elijah bowed in prayer, asking even more earnestly
that the rain might come. Then he sent his servant a second
time to look over the sea. But the sky was still cloudless.

Six times this happened, and yet there was no sign that
his prayer had been heard.

When the servant went the seventh time to look, he re-

36

turned excitedly, saying, "Behold, there ariseth a little cloud out of the sea, like a man's hand."

That was enough for Elijah. He needed no other token. Small as the cloud was—only the size of a man's hand in the great vault of heaven—he was sure it was God's answer. He could almost feel the rain already.

"Hurry!" he said to his servant. "Go to Ahab and say to him, Prepare thy chariot, and get thee down, that the rain stop thee not."

As Elijah followed his servant down the mountainside the tiny cloud grew swiftly larger and larger, till "the heaven was black with clouds and wind, and there was a great rain."

The storm and the darkness caught up with Ahab as he fled in his chariot for shelter. The deluge soaked him to the skin, the wild wind tore at his clothing, the crashing thunder frightened his horses as they dashed onward through the night.

Suddenly, as a flash of lightning threw a bright, swift glare across the storm-swept countryside, the worried king saw a figure running ahead of his chariot. Who could it be?

Another flash. Again he glimpsed the figure. The man was still running, seemingly without effort, and as fast as the horses. Now Ahab recognized him. Elijah! The man of the mountaintop! The man of the fire and the rain! The man of God! Guiding him home through the dark!

"And the hand of the Lord was on Elijah; and he . . . ran before Ahab to the entrance of Jezreel."

STORY 7

The Still Small Voice

≈≈≈≈≈≈≈≈≈≈≈≈≈

ELIJAH must have been very tired after all the excitement of that great day on Carmel, besides running all that way to Jezreel in front of Ahab's chariot. And being so tired, he wasn't ready for the shock that came to him next day.

He was still resting when a messenger arrived from Queen Jezebel, who had just heard from Ahab what had happened to the prophets of Baal. She had not been on Mount Carmel; she had not seen the fire fall from heaven; so she refused to believe that the breaking of the drought had anything to do with Elijah or his God. Furious that her prophets had been killed, she sent this message: "So let the gods do to me, and more also, if I make not thy life as the life of one of them by to morrow about this time."

Sudden fear seized Elijah. Forgetting that God could have cared for him just as well in Jezreel as He had by the brook Cherith, or on the top of Mount Carmel, "he arose, and

went for his life, and came to Beer-sheba, which belongeth to Judah."

Two hundred miles he fled from this angry woman. Indeed, not until he had crossed the boundary between Israel and Judah did he begin to feel safe again. Then, leaving his servant in Beersheba, he went on alone "a day's journey into the wilderness, and came and sat down under a juniper tree."

By this time he was completely worn out. His spirits were so low that he even prayed that he might die. Then he fell asleep.

"And as he lay and slept . . . an angel touched him, and said unto him, Arise and eat."

God had not forgotten His weary servant, though he had run away from danger.

Waking, Elijah looked around him and saw "a cake baken on the coals, and a cruse of water at his head. And he did eat and drink, and laid him down again."

How long he slept nobody knows. It may well have been for hours, so tired was he. Then "the angel of the Lord came

again the second time, and touched him, and said, Arise and eat; because the journey is too great for thee."

So Elijah found a second meal awaiting him in the desert. As he ate he must have thought how wonderful it was that God knew where he was, and where he was going; that God knew he would find no food on the way; and that God knew that such a journey was too great for his strength!

Gratefully Elijah "did eat and drink, and went in the strength of that meat forty days and forty nights unto Horeb the mount of God."

All his life he had wanted to see Horeb, where so many wonderful things had happened to the children of Israel in the long ago. He knew it was called "the mount of God," and he hoped that perhaps he might come closer to God there than he had ever been before.

"My God is Jehovah!" he whispered to himself as he journeyed on from day to day over the trackless wilderness. "My God is Jehovah! But will I see Him when I reach His mount; will I hear His voice?"

At last he arrived, and stood in awe upon the historic mountain. Horeb at last! Here, where Moses had stood! Here, where God had spoken alone with His faithful servant when Israel came out of Egypt! But where was God now?

Suddenly a great wind came up, far greater than the one that had brought the rain to Carmel. It roared up the ravines and churned the dust of the desert into clouds. Picking up great rocks as if with invisible hands, it dashed them to pieces against the mountainside.

41

Afraid of the threats of the angry queen Jezebel Elijah escaped into the wilderness and wished that he might die, but God sent His angel to encourage His faithful prophet.

But "the Lord was not in the wind."

Soon the earth began to tremble. Cracks opened in the earth. Elijah had never known such a quake. But "the Lord was not in the earthquake."

Then the sky glowed as fire burst out on the mountaintop. Elijah remembered the story of how fire and smoke had covered the mount when God gave Israel the Ten Commandments; "but the Lord was not in the fire."

Then where was He?

Very near indeed, much nearer than Elijah dreamed.

As the prophet sheltered in a cave, he presently heard a "still small voice."

Could this be God? He had thought the mighty God of heaven might be in the hurricane, in the earthquake, or in the raging fire, but not in a voice so soft and gentle as this. Yet as he listened he felt the power of God in the words that were spoken, for God asked him one simple question, "What doest thou here, Elijah?"

He had not expected this. He had come all this way to commune with God and worship Him, not to answer questions.

42

But he knew what God meant. He knew God was saying to him, "Why aren't you in Jezreel standing for Me before that wicked Jezebel? Why did you run away from her? Why did you not stay and follow up the victory I gave you on Carmel? Elijah, O Elijah, why did you fail Me?"

That still small voice moved the prophet more than all else he had seen and heard on Horeb. He began to excuse and pity himself. "I, even I only, am left," he said; "and they seek my life, to take it away."

"No," God said to him. "I have left me seven thousand in Israel, all the knees which have not bowed unto Baal." The suggestion was, *"They* haven't run away."

Then God told him to return to his post of duty. On his way he was to anoint Hazael to be king over Syria, Jehu to be king over Israel, and Elisha—yes, Elisha—to take his place as the prophet of the Lord.

As he journeyed northward toward Damascus, Elijah thought again and again of what had happened at Horeb. How could he ever forget it? The farther he traveled, the louder grew the still small voice, until it seemed to shout above the roar of earthquake, wind, and fire. "Go, return! Go, return! . . . and Elisha . . . shalt thou anoint to be prophet in thy room."

Thus had God spoken. Humbly Elijah proceeded to obey.

STORY 8

The Stolen Vineyard

KING AHAB was a very rich man, as wealth was counted in his day. He owned at least two palaces, one in Samaria and one in Jezreel. The one in Samaria was known as the "ivory house," its walls being covered with slabs of polished ivory cut from the tusks of elephants.

But with all his riches Ahab was not a happy man. Like many boys and girls today, he was always wanting more. If someone had something better than he possessed, he felt envious and miserable.

One day, looking out of the window of his palace in Jezreel, his eyes roamed over a beautiful vineyard that adjoined the royal lands. The thought occurred to him that it would make a fine addition to the palace gardens, and he made up his mind to buy it.

Going to the owner, whose name was Naboth, he offered to give him another vineyard in exchange for this one, or, if he preferred, to pay "the worth of it in money."

44

THE STOLEN VINEYARD

It was a fair enough offer, but Naboth didn't want to sell. The vineyard had been his father's, he said, and his grandfather's. Indeed, it had belonged to his family for more years than he could tell, and he couldn't bring himself to part with it.

At this, Ahab was very much upset, and when he got back to his palace he behaved like a spoiled child. Throwing himself on his bed, he turned his face to the wall and refused to eat.

When he didn't come down to dinner that evening Queen Jezebel went to his room to find out what was the matter.

"Why are you so sad?" she asked. "Why won't you eat?"

Then he told her how he had offered to buy Naboth's vineyard and the man had refused to sell it.

Jezebel scoffed. "That's a fine thing to be miserable about!" she said, in other words. "Aren't you king? Can't you do what you like? Get up! Eat and be merry! If you want that vineyard, I'll get it for you."

Ahab did as he was told, and Jezebel set about getting the vineyard for him in her own wicked way.

She wrote to the heads of the city council and told them to "proclaim a fast, and set Naboth on high among the people." They were then to call in two false witnesses who would testify that Naboth had blasphemed God and the king. After hearing the evidence they were to find Naboth guilty and have him stoned to death.

It was as simple as that, and as evil. With all the city officials already sold out to Jezebel, and afraid of their lives, poor Naboth didn't have a chance.

The court was summoned. The two witnesses came in and accused Naboth of blasphemy. In vain he protested his innocence; in vain he swore he had never uttered blasphemy in all his life, either against God or the king. The judges accepted the testimony of the two witnesses, and condemned him to death. He was then carried out of the city and stoned.

But if Jezebel and Ahab thought they were going to get away with this wicked murder, they were mistaken.

The very day that Ahab walked into Naboth's vineyard to take possession of it, who should be there but Elijah, whom he had last seen running before his chariot on that stormy night after fire had fallen from heaven on Mount Carmel and the prophets of Baal had been slain.

46

"Hast thou found me, O mine enemy?" he cried in a startled voice.

"I have found thee," replied Elijah, sternly: "because thou hast sold thyself to work evil in the sight of the Lord."

"Thus saith the Lord, Hast thou killed, and also taken possession? . . . In the place where the dogs licked the blood of Naboth shall dogs lick thy blood, even thine."

Concerning Jezebel, he said, "The dogs shall eat Jezebel by the walls of Jezreel."

Elijah could not have spoken more frankly. Certainly Ahab was left in no doubt as to what God thought of the murder of Naboth. We may be sure that he never got one moment's pleasure out of that stolen vineyard. Every time he walked in it he must have wondered whether Elijah was hiding somewhere among the vines, waiting to condemn him again for his evil deed. Every time he looked at it from his palace window he must have thought of the price both he and Jezebel would have to pay for it someday.

Such is the bitter fruit of envy, jealousy, and selfishness.

STORY 9

Elijah's Prophecy Comes True

AHAB did not live very long after he stole Naboth's vineyard. For a while he was sorry for his sin, but he could neither give the vineyard back to the dead man nor forget the great wrong he had done.

Some time later Jehoshaphat, king of Judah, came on a state visit to Samaria. A great feast was held in honor of the occasion. The two kings, clad in their royal robes, sat on thrones placed outside the city gate. They talked of many things, but chiefly about the city of Ramoth-gilead which, Ahab said, belonged to Israel but was now occupied by the Syrians. Would Jehoshaphat help him get it back?

"I am as thou art, my people as thy people, my horses as thy horses," said Jehoshaphat with great courtesy; "but, well, hadn't we better ask the Lord about it?"

Ahab called for his "prophets." They came, hundreds of them, and said exactly what he wanted them to say: "Go up; for the Lord shall deliver it into the hand of the king."

One man even put iron horns on his head and said, "Thus saith the Lord, With these shalt thou push the Syrians, until thou have consumed them."

But Jehoshaphat didn't like the look of these men. "Is there not here a prophet of the Lord besides," he said, "that we might inquire of *him?*"

"There is yet one man, Micaiah," said Ahab testily; "but I hate him; for he doth not prophesy good concerning me, but evil."

"Don't say that," said Jehoshaphat. "Call him."

So Micaiah was called, and he gave warning in the name of the Lord that the plan would fail.

"I saw all Israel scattered upon the hills, as sheep that have not a shepherd," he said.

"There," said Ahab to Jehoshaphat. "Didn't I tell you that he would prophesy no good concerning me, but evil?"

"Your prophets are lying," said Micaiah; "the Lord has spoken evil concerning you."

At this the man wearing the iron horns slapped Micaiah on the cheek, while Ahab said, "Put this fellow in the prison, and feed him with bread of affliction and with water of affliction, until I come in peace."

As the soldiers led him away, Micaiah cried, "If you return at all in peace, the Lord has not spoken by me."

Ahab didn't want to hear the truth, and Jehoshaphat was led astray by him. The two kings marched on Ramoth-gilead,

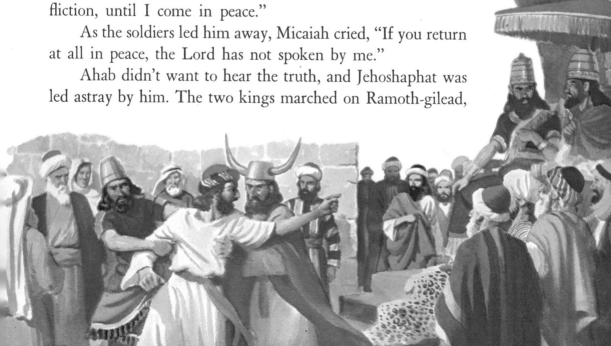

but their armies were defeated and scattered like sheep without a shepherd, just as Micaiah had said.

Jehoshaphat escaped with his life, but Ahab was killed.

"A certain man drew a bow at a venture, and smote the king of Israel between the joints of the harness," wounding him seriously.

Ahab's servants propped him up so that it would look as though he were still fighting, but so much blood poured from his wound that it covered the bottom of his chariot, and he died at sundown that evening.

They brought the dead king back to Samaria and buried him there. As Ahab's chariot and armor were being washed in the pool of Samaria, dogs came and licked up his blood.

So Elijah's prophecy was fulfilled.

As for Jezebel, she lived twelve years after Ahab's death, but the day came when her own guards threw her out of the window of the palace in Jezreel, where she once plotted the death of Naboth. "And some of her blood was sprinkled on the wall, and on the horses." Afterward, when they came to bury her, "they found no more of her than the skull, and the feet, and the palms of her hands." The dogs had eaten the rest of her, just as Elijah long years before had said they would.

It is well to remember that God always means what He says. His prophecies and His promises always come to pass.

STORY 10

Fate of the Three Captains

AFTER Ahab's death his son Ahaziah became king of Israel. Sad to say, he was no better than his father or his mother, and "served Baal, and worshiped him, and provoked to anger the Lord God of Israel."

One day he met with a serious accident, falling out of an upper window in the palace. It seems that the wooden lattice must have given way as he leaned against it.

How badly he was hurt we are not told, but it was enough to make him worry whether or not he would get better.

Anxious to learn his fate, he sent messengers to inquire of Baalzebub, the god of Ekron, just as though this wooden idol would know what was going to happen to him.

On their way the messengers met Elijah, though they did not recognize him. He asked them sternly why they were going to seek help from Baalzebub rather than from the God of heaven. Then he ordered them to turn back and tell Ahaziah that he was going to die.

So frightened were they by the old prophet that they obeyed him.

Ahaziah was surprised to see them back so soon. When they told him what had happened, he asked them to describe the man who had spoken to them.

"He wore a garment of haircloth," they said, "with a girdle of leather about his loins."

They did not need to say more.

"It is Elijah the Tishbite!" said Ahaziah.

Then he sent one of his captains with fifty men to seize Elijah and bring him to Samaria.

The captain found the prophet sitting on a hilltop, and ordered him to come down at once. "Thou man of God," he cried, "the king hath said, Come down!"

Elijah refused. He felt that this was no way for these godless soldiers of a godless king to treat the prophet of the Lord.

"If I be a man of God," he said, "then let fire come down from heaven, and consume thee and thy fifty."

A moment later there was a sudden blaze of light as fire fell from heaven and the men vanished.

When the king heard what had happened, he was outraged, and sent a second captain with another fifty men to capture Elijah and bring him to court.

Elijah was still on the hilltop, quite undisturbed.

"Come down quickly!" ordered the captain of the second fifty. "King's orders!"

Once again Elijah said, "If I be a man of God, let fire

come down from heaven, and consume thee and thy fifty."
Again fire fell from heaven, and the captain and his men were
consumed.

When news of this reached Ahaziah he sent a third
captain with fifty men to take Elijah. This captain, however,
had learned something from the sad fate of his friends. When
he came to the hill where Elijah was sitting he "fell on his
knees before Elijah, and besought him, and said unto him,
O man of God, I pray thee, let my life, and the life of these
fifty thy servants, be precious in thy sight."

God appreciated the humble attitude of this man, and the respect he paid to His prophet. "Go down with him," He told Elijah: "be not afraid of him."

So Elijah went with this captain and his fifty men and came to the palace where Ahaziah was lying in bed.

Elijah showed no fear of the king, though he was now within his power and could so easily have been thrown into a dungeon any minute. Nor did he change his message. Instead, he told the king, as he had already told his messengers, that because he had sent for help to Baalzebub the god of Ekron, rather than to the God of heaven, he would not recover from his sickness, but would surely die.

And die he did, just as Elijah had said. Not only, of course, because he had sent to inquire of Baalzebub, but because all his life—just like his father and mother—he had hated Jehovah and served the gods of the heathen.

STORY 11

Heaven's Fiery Chariot

ELIJAH'S work was almost done. In a very evil time he had stood for God the best he knew how. Bravely he had fought God's battles and championed His cause. In his heart he felt that God was about to call him away from this world.

Elisha was with him constantly now, for Elijah was getting the young man ready to take over his work when he should have to leave it. Elisha, you remember, was mentioned by "the still small voice" as the one to take Elijah's place. Elijah had anointed him on his return from Mount Horeb, and the two had been working together ever since.

As they drew near to Bethel the "sons of the prophets" came out to meet them. These were young men from one of the schools of the prophets Elijah is believed to have started.

Strangely, these young people had the same idea about Elijah—that he would not be around much longer. They asked Elisha if God was going to take his master away soon.

"Yea, I know it; hold ye your peace," he said to them, not wanting to talk about it.

Then Elijah told Elisha to wait at Bethel while he went on by himself. "The Lord hath sent me to Jericho," he said.

Elisha refused to let him go alone. "As the Lord liveth, and as thy soul liveth," he said, "I will not leave thee."

So the two went on together to Jericho, where there was another school of the prophets. Here again the young men came out to meet them, and again they warned Elisha that he would soon be losing his master.

"Yea, I know it," he said to them; "hold ye your peace."

Elijah then told Elisha to wait at Jericho while he went on over Jordan. Again Elisha refused. He had made up his mind to stay with his master to the very end, not knowing when or how that would be.

"As the Lord liveth, and as thy soul liveth, I will not leave thee," he said.

So the two went on toward Jordan, while at least fifty young men from the school followed at a distance to see what might happen.

They saw plenty. When Elijah and Elisha reached the river they did not wait for a boat to ferry them across. Taking off his mantle, Elijah folded it and "smote the waters, and they were divided hither and thither, so that they two went over on dry ground."

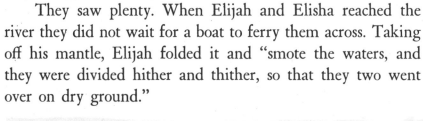

If the young people thought that they might follow, they were mistaken, for the water quickly flowed together again. A moment later the Jordan looked the same as ever.

On the other side Elijah turned to Elisha and said, very tenderly, "Ask what I shall do for thee, before I be taken away from thee."

The dreaded moment of parting had come! Soon Elijah would be gone forever. What should Elisha ask of him? Money? Land? Houses? Position? Anything he might desire could be his, for surely Elijah was going straight to heaven.

"And Elisha said, I pray thee, let a double portion of thy spirit be upon me."

He could not have made a better choice. God must have been as pleased with him as He had been with Solomon when he asked for wisdom.

Elijah said it was a hard thing he had asked—for of course only God could give His Spirit—but, he added, "if you see me being taken, it shall be so."

Then they walked on together. "They went on, and talked," the Bible says, and it is a pity we do not know the last precious words these two great men of God said to each other. No doubt Elijah urged Elisha to be true and loyal to God and keep the good work going which he had started.

They were now not far from Pisgah, which is but ten miles from Jericho. Perhaps they even climbed to the top, to the place where Moses died and God raised him from the dead.

By and by the wind began to blow, harder and harder, with a twisting, swirling motion. Elijah seemed to be caught up in it and lifted above the earth. Suddenly a blaze of light surrounded them as something appeared in the sky, like one of Ahab's chariots, only ten thousand times more glorious. It was shining radiantly as though it were on fire, while the creatures that drew it seemed to be on fire too. Surely it must be one of God's own chariots, a chariot of angels, sent to bring his faithful servant home! Swiftly it approached Elijah, who stepped into it, and was gone.

"And Elijah went up by a whirlwind into heaven."

"My father, my father!" cried Elisha as he saw his beloved master carried swiftly upward in this blaze of glory. "The chariot of Israel, and the horsemen thereof!"

Something fell from the chariot as it sped away. Slowly it billowed down to earth as the wind subsided. Eagerly Elisha

ran to pick it up. It was a mantle, Elijah's mantle, the prophet's last gift to his friend.

Picking it up, Elisha returned to the Jordan, beyond which was Jericho, with its school of the prophets, and beyond that, the great work God wanted him to do throughout all Israel.

Could he do this work? Was he prepared for it? Could he be the leader Elijah had been? Would God indeed give him a double portion of His Spirit?

The Jordan was his first test. Would it open for him as it had for Elijah?

Taking Elijah's mantle, he smote the water as his master had done, crying, "Where is the Lord God of Elijah?" The river parted and Elisha went over. Now he knew for sure that God was with him and always would be.

The sons of the prophets were watching. At first they thought Elijah must have returned; but no, Elisha was alone. Then they knew they had a new master. "The spirit of Elijah doth rest on Elisha," they said.

And they were right. For Elisha went on to do more and greater miracles than even Elijah had done.

PART II

Stories of Elisha

(2 KINGS 2:16-13:20)

STORY 1

Bad Boys and the Bears

ELISHA did his best to explain what had happened to Elijah, but people wouldn't believe him. Even the young men in the school of the prophets at Jericho found it hard to understand how their beloved master could have been taken up to heaven in a chariot of fire and a whirlwind. They were sure that, even so, he must have fallen somewhere, maybe "upon some mountain, or into some valley," and they wanted to go and search for him.

Elisha told them not to, for they would only waste their time. But they went just the same, all fifty of them. Three days they sought for Elijah, but without success.

One day the elders of the city of Jericho came to Elisha and asked him if he could do something about their water supply. It had a bad taste, they said, and was no good for irrigation. Plants wouldn't grow in it.

Elisha was glad to help. He called for a vessel full of salt, and took it to the place where the spring bubbled out of

63

When the water of the city of Jericho became bitter and unfit for use, Elisha called for some salt which he poured into the source of the stream, and God made the water good to drink.

the ground. Pouring in the salt, he said, "Thus saith the Lord, I have healed these waters; there shall not be from thence any more death or barren land. So the waters were healed unto this day."

That stream is still flowing and the water is still sweet. I know, for I drank some of it one day when visiting there some years ago.

Leaving the people of Jericho very happy, Elisha made his way back to Bethel. As he approached the city, to his surprise there came running toward him a group of unruly boys, shouting, "Go up, thou bald head; go up, thou bald head!"

So his story of Elijah's translation had reached here already! And this was what the people thought of it! Clearly they didn't believe a word of his report. They were laughing at the idea of anybody's going up to heaven in a fiery chariot. These rude youngsters were actually telling him to go up there, too.

Elisha saw that it was all part of a plan to wreck his work. His enemies wanted to make him the laughingstock of the country. He could not permit it. Nor could he allow so solemn,

so beautiful an event as his master's triumphal entry into heaven to be made a subject of scornful mirth. This was too much. These bad boys must be taught a lesson.

So as the crowd of scoffing youngsters followed him chanting, "Go up, thou bald head!" Elisha "turned back and looked on them, and cursed them in the name of the Lord." In other words, he asked God to deal with them as He saw fit.

As he did so, two she-bears came slinking out of the nearby woods.

Suddenly the mocking ceased, and laughter turned to screams of terror as the boys fled for their lives. But the bears caught up with them and mauled forty-two of them. How badly they were hurt we are not told, but it is safe to say they all learned a lesson that day which they never forgot. Never again would they treat a man of God with disrespect.

Meanwhile Elisha went on his way and came to Mount Carmel, where God had come so near to his master, and fire had fallen from heaven. It was a good place to go to at the beginning of his ministry.

STORY 2

Valley of Red Ditches

FROM Mount Carmel Elisha went to Samaria. He traveled a great deal, much as Elijah had done before him, not stopping very long in any one place.

One day there was a loud knocking on the door of the humble cottage where he was staying. Going to see who was there, he found a crowd of armed men outside. In their midst were two royal figures in fine armor.

He recognized them at once. The old, bearded man was Jehoshaphat, king of Judah. The other was young Jehoram, king of Israel, who had ascended the throne when his brother Ahaziah fell out of the palace window and died from his injuries. A son of Ahab, he was as wicked as his father.

The two kings said that they had come to talk with Elisha about an important matter.

Suddenly turning on Jehoram, Elisha asked what he meant by coming to a prophet of the Lord. "Go to your own prophets!" he said to him; "the prophets of your father and mother."

66

VALLEY OF RED DITCHES

"If it were not for the presence of Jehoshaphat, king of Judah," he added, "I wouldn't even look at you or see you."

It was hardly a tactful way to talk to a king, but Elisha was a very brave man, and he wanted Jehoram to know that he strongly disapproved of his evil ways.

Because good King Jehoshaphat was there, Elisha agreed to listen to their story. They were both in great trouble. Their armies had started out to fight the Moabites. Thinking to surprise them by attacking from the east, they had taken a long detour through desert country, and now were out of water, with nothing to drink for man or beast. They were at the mercy of their enemies. What should they do now? Had Elisha anything to suggest?

Elisha called for a minstrel, and while sweet music was being played "the hand of the Lord came upon him. And he said, Thus saith the Lord, Make this valley full of ditches. For thus saith the Lord, Ye shall not see wind, neither shall ye see rain; yet that valley shall be filled with water, that ye may drink, both ye, and your cattle, and your beasts. And this is but a light thing in the sight of the Lord: he will deliver the Moabites also into your hand."

I can almost hear Jehoram scoffing, "Dig ditches in a dry valley! What an idea!" But Jehoshaphat believed God's

prophet, and the ditches were dug. Those ditches proved his faith.

Early next morning the sun rose in a cloudless sky. The air was still, and there was no sign of rain; but suddenly down one of the mountain ravines "by the way of Edom" came a raging stream of water. It spread over the valley floor and filled the ditches to overflowing. Soldiers, horses, and cattle drank greedily, and their strength revived.

By this time, of course, the Moabites were awake and ready for battle. Looking eastward, they saw the soldiers of Israel behaving in a very strange manner. While some were standing, others were kneeling, and still others were lying flat on their stomachs. And there was blood all about them, or so it seemed, as the early morning sun was reflected from the water-filled ditches.

"Look! They are killing one another!" they cried, and dashed down the mountainside to finish off the invaders of their country.

Of course, they had made a dreadful mistake. When they reached the ditches they found they were full of water, not blood. Maybe some of them fell into the ditches and were drowned. Anyhow, the Israelites had seen them coming and were ready for them. Thanks to the God of Elisha, what might have been a bad defeat was turned into a great victory.

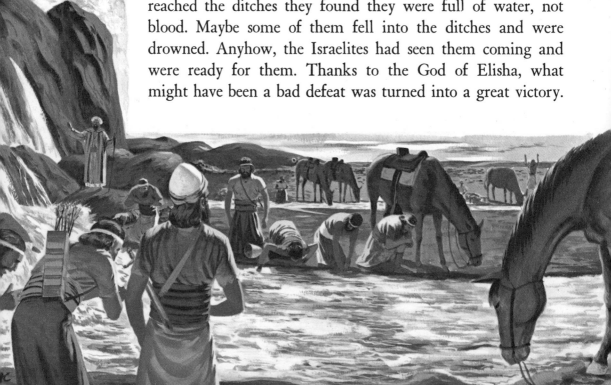

STORY 3

Mother's Mysterious Oil Pots

ABOUT this time one of the "sons of the prophets" died, leaving a widow with two young sons. The Bible doesn't tell us the boys' names, so I am sure nobody will mind if I call them Jonas and Joel.

So poor was the little family that there wasn't a cent in the house. Worse than that, their father had been heavily in debt, and now the creditor wanted his money.

Their mother told the creditor she couldn't let him have what he claimed; she just didn't have it. So he said he would take Jonas and Joel and sell them as slaves to pay the bill.

Poor little Mother! How sad and frightened she must have been! But what could she do? Where could she turn for help? Then she thought of Elisha.

Leaving the two boys at home, she went in search of the prophet, hoping against hope that he would show her a way out of her trouble.

At last she found him and told her story.

69

"Tell me," said Elisha kindly, "what do you have in your house?"

"Nothing," said the poor widow. "Nothing, that is, except a pot of oil."

Then Elisha told her to do a strange thing. "Go, borrow . . . vessels abroad of all thy neighbours, even empty vessels; borrow not a few."

He must have noticed the questioning look on the widow's face, for he went on to tell her what to do with the empty oil pots. After she had gathered all she could find, she was to shut the door of her house and start pouring oil into them out of her pot. And she was to keep on pouring until all the vessels were full.

The widow must have wondered for a moment whether the man of God was serious. She knew she had just one pot of oil, and how could that one pot fill many empty pots? And what would the neighbors think if she started asking them for all their crockery?

On the way home she must have questioned whether or not she should do as Elisha had said. Nobody likes to look silly before his friends, and this could make her appear very silly indeed if it didn't work. Imagine the kitchen floor covered with empty oil pots, and nothing happening to them!

She decided she would do as she had been told, and trust the God of Elisha.

"Jonas," she said, on reaching home, "please go next door and ask Mrs. Isaacson for a couple of empty oil pots; and Joel, you go up the road and ask Mrs. Naomi for all she can spare."

"Why, Mother?"

"Never mind, dears. Go and fetch them. Then ask all the other neighbors for every pot they will let me have."

As the boys ran off they no doubt wondered what was happening to Mother. Perhaps the worry of Father's death had been too much for her. But they went for the pots just the same.

Soon they were back, carrying all the pots they could. Then they ran off for more.

The neighbors, looking out of their windows, began to wonder what was going on. "Why are those boys taking all those oil pots down to their house?" they asked themselves. When they asked Jonas and Joel, the only answer they got was, "Dunno; Mother just wants them for something."

When the kitchen floor was just about covered with pots Mother shut the door.

"What are you going to do with them all?" asked Jonas and Joel, amused.

"Never mind; just watch and see."

Then she picked up her one precious pot with the oil in it. With a prayer in her heart, "Dear God, make it work!" she began to pour.

71

MOTHER'S MYSTERIOUS OIL POTS

The first pot wasn't too big a worry, for she was just pouring from one to another; but the second!

She felt her own pot; it was still heavy. She looked into it; there was still some oil there. She began to pour into the second pot. Soon it, too, was filled to the brim. Eagerly she turned to the third pot, the fourth, the fifth, the sixth. Then she lost count.

With their eyes popping out, the boys looked on in amazement.

"But where's it coming from, Mother?"

"I don't know!" she cried as she went on pouring. "I don't know!"

Row after row of pots was filled. Suddenly she noticed that she had reached the last pot.

"Jonas, Joel!" she cried. "More pots! Get me another pot quickly!"

They ran up the street, knocking excitedly on all the doors.

"Mother wants another pot! Mother wants another pot!"

But there were no more pots to be had.

"And the oil stayed."

Leaving the boys to look after the precious oil, Mother ran to Elisha and gasped out her wonderful story, her heart overflowing with gratitude to God for His goodness.

There must have been a lovely smile on Elisha's face as he listened. Then he said to her, "Go, sell the oil, and pay thy debt, and live thou and thy children on the rest."

God loves to do things like this for those who trust Him.

With her heart overflowing to God for His goodness, the poor widow began pouring the oil into the vessels as Elisha had told her, and it continued to flow until every jar was full.

STORY 4

Kindness Repaid

A S ELISHA journeyed here and there through Palestine he often passed through a place called Shunem, where lived a very wealthy lady. Sometimes he would stop at her home and ask for something to eat. Always he was invited in and well fed, and always he left a blessing behind him when he went on his way.

The great lady was much impressed by Elisha. He was so courteous, so friendly, so reverent, so different from men of the world, that she said to her husband one day, "I perceive that this is an holy man of God, which passeth by us continually."

She proposed that they build a little room in which he could rest, and put in it "a bed, and a table, and a stool, and a candlestick."

Her husband agreed. The room was built and furnished, and the next time Elisha arrived he was shown into it. How pleased and thankful he was!

Nobody had ever been so kind to him before.

Next day he told his servant Gehazi to call the lady before him that he might express his gratitude. "Say now unto her, Behold, thou hast been careful for us with all this care; what is to be done for thee?"

He offered to speak to the king, or the captain of the army, for her if she had any favor to ask of them, but she said No, she was content. Then he said to Gehazi, "What *can* we do for her?"

Gehazi thought it over. By and by he came up with a bright idea.

"She has no child, and her husband is old," he said.

"Aha!" said Elisha, grateful for the suggestion. "Call her."

When the lady came this time, Elisha promised that before a year had passed she would have a son.

"Impossible!" she said.

But nothing is impossible with God. At the very time Elisha said, the little boy was born.

Needless to say, the lady loved her son very dearly and

watched over him night and day as he grew up. No doubt Elisha took a lot of interest in him, too, as he visited the family from time to time.

Then one hot summer day, when the boy was out in the harvest field with his father, he suddenly cried out, "My head! My head!" Perhaps he had sunstroke. Anyhow, his father became very worried, and said to one of his servants, "Carry him to his mother."

She took him on her lap and held him there till noon, when he died. Then she carried the limp little body upstairs to the room she had made for Elisha, and laid it on his bed. Closing the door behind her, she went out with aching heart and tear-drenched face.

But she wiped away the tears, and putting on a brave face, asked her husband for a servant and one of the asses, that she might go at once to Elisha.

He wanted to know why. "It is neither new moon, nor Sabbath," he said.

She didn't tell him why, perhaps lest the shock be too

76

great for him if he should find his little son was dead.

Saddling the ass herself, she said to the servant, "Drive, and go forward; slack not thy riding for me, except I bid thee."

So they went at full speed to Mount Carmel where they found Elisha.

Falling at his feet, she told all that had happened, and about the cold little form that lay on his bed.

Elisha was shocked. Handing his staff to Gehazi, he told him to hurry with all speed to the dead child and lay the staff upon his face.

Gehazi ran on his mission, and Elisha followed, the anxious mother at his side.

By and by the two saw Gehazi returning, looking sad and worried.

"The child is not awaked," he said.

Elisha was worried now.

Arriving at the house, he went upstairs, entered his room, shut the door, and "prayed unto the Lord."

What a prayer was that! How he must have implored the great and wonderful God whom he served to honor his faith and restore the little boy to life!

Then, he "lay upon the child, and put his mouth upon his mouth, and his eyes upon his eyes, and his hands upon his hands: and he stretched himself upon the child; and the flesh of the child waxed warm."

Yet that warmth was all he noticed; there was no other sign of life.

Elisha left the room and "walked in the house to and fro," wondering what more he could do. But his faith was still strong that God could raise the dead—and would.

As he paced up and down he prayed ever more urgently that God would do this wonderful thing for the glory of His name and the blessing of this dear woman who had been so kind to him.

Then he went back to his room. The little lad still lay motionless upon the bed. He stretched himself upon him once more. Suddenly the child awoke, sneezed seven times, and opened his eyes.

The miracle had happened!

Calling the mother, Elisha said kindly, with deep happiness in his voice, "Take up thy son."

Overjoyed, she fell at the prophet's feet and poured out her thanks. Then she picked up her boy, hugging and kissing him as only a mother could who had just seen her dearest treasure brought back from the dead.

STORY 5

Faithful Little Maid

LET me go! Let me go!" screamed the little maid. "Don't take me away from my mother!"

But the cruel raiders took no notice of her cries. They threw her on a horse behind a big, burly Syrian soldier and set out for Damascus.

Weeping all the way, the little maid sobbed out between her tears, "Why did God let this happen to me? Why? Why? Why?"

In the big city she was sold as a slave, and became the servant of the wife of Naaman, captain of the host of the king of Syria.

How homesick and hopeless she must have felt that first night in the big house, with all those strange people! Yet she didn't forget to say her prayers. Her parents had brought her up to love the God of heaven, and she made up her mind she would be true to Him whatever might happen.

Fortunately her mistress was kind to her. Soon they were

talking together like mother and daughter. No doubt the
little maid told some of the stories her real mother had told
her about the wonderful way the God of heaven had cared
for Israel in years gone by—stories like the one about the
crossing of the Red Sea, which every Hebrew child knew
by heart.

Often the little maid noticed that her mistress had a
very sad look on her face. She wondered why, but didn't dare
to ask. Then one day she found out what the trouble was.
Naaman, her husband, had that most dreaded disease, leprosy.

The little maid had seen lepers before, and knew the
awful things the disease did to them. Her kind heart went
out in sympathy to her master and mistress. She longed to do
something to help them, but what could a little girl do, so
far from home in a strange, strange land?

Then she had a bright idea. If *she* couldn't help, maybe
God could.

Seeing her mistress in tears, she went to her and said,
very gently, "Would God my lord were with the prophet that

80

is in Samaria! for he would recover him of his leprosy."

"Sweet child, what makes you think that?" asked her mistress.

This gave the little maid her chance. She began to talk about all the wonderful things Elisha had done, and Elijah before him.

"Why, the other day Elisha raised a dead boy to life. Yes, he was quite dead. Everybody says so. And once he made the bitter spring of Jericho sweet. And his master, Elijah, did some wonderful things too. He made a poor widow's barrel of meal and cruse of oil last many days, maybe a whole year. Once he even brought fire down from heaven on the top of Mount Carmel, and burned up the sacrifice even though it was soaking wet with water. Oh, yes, my lady, the God of heaven is a wonderful God. And Elisha is His prophet, a man of God. I'm sure he would heal your husband if he'd just go to see him."

So she talked. On and on. The Bible says, "Thus and thus said the maid." How much that "thus and thus" covers!

Her mistress was so touched that she told the whole story to a servant, who went and told it to Naaman. He was so impressed that he told the king of Syria, who thought the child had a fine idea, and said he would write to the king of Israel about it at once.

Unfortunately the king of Syria got things a bit mixed up. By the time the little maid's story reached him, he thought it was the king of Israel, not Elisha, who was to do the healing; and he put this in his letter. He wrote: "I have . . . sent

Naaman my servant to thee, that thou mayest recover him of his leprosy."

When the king of Israel received the letter and learned that Naaman had already arrived with "ten talents of silver, and six thousand pieces of gold, and ten changes of raiment" to pay for his cure, he almost went out of his mind. The Bible says he tore his clothes and cried out, "Am I God, to kill and make alive, that this man doth send unto me to recover a man of his leprosy? . . . See how he seeketh a quarrel against me."

Soon the story was all over Samaria. It reached Elisha, who must have smiled at the fix in which the idolatrous king now found himself. He could have left him to find his own way out but, seeing an opportunity to bring glory to God

in a foreign land, he told the king to send Naaman to him.

"So Naaman came with his horses and with his chariot, and stood at the door of the house of Elisha."

Elisha sent a messenger to say that if he would wash in the Jordan seven times, he would be cured of his leprosy.

At this Naaman became very angry and rode away, saying to his servants, "I thought, He will surely come out to me, and stand, and call on the name of the Lord his God, and strike his hand over the place, and recover the leper."

He was upset because no great fuss had been made of him—and worse, because his national pride had been hurt. Why should he go and wash in Jordan? "Are not Abana and Pharpar, rivers of Damascus, better than all the waters of Israel?" he snapped. "May I not wash in *them,* and be clean?"

His servants had more sense. They said to him, "If the prophet had asked you to do some great thing, wouldn't you have done it? Why not obey when he suggests something so simple as, Wash and be clean?"

At last Naaman saw light in what they said. Turning his chariot around, he drove down toward the Jordan. It was a rough, bumpy journey, and many times he must have wondered whether it was worth while. Perhaps, after all, the prophet was just playing with him because he was a foreign general.

Arriving at the Jordan, he took off his clothes and waded in, while his servants watched to see what would happen. Then

83

he dipped under the water and waded out. All looked at the white spot that marked the place where the leprosy had started. It was still there.

He waded in the second time and out again. Still nothing happened.

He went in the third time, the fourth, the fifth, the sixth, and still the horrid mark was there.

All the servants had been counting. All knew that the next time would be the seventh, and the last.

Once more Naaman entered the water, dipped, and came out.

"Look! Look!" he cried. "It's gone!"

All crowded round. It was true. The leprosy had disappeared.

Throwing on his clothes, Naaman leaped into his chariot. How he drove up that mountain road! It's a wonder the wheels didn't come off as they sank in the ruts and bumped against the rocks.

His servants followed at the same wild speed. At last they came to Elisha's house.

This time he was there to greet them, for he guessed what had happened when he heard the galloping hoofs.

Scarcely knowing how to express his gratitude, Naaman bowed his head and said, "Now I know that there is no God in all the earth, but in Israel."

So the little captive maid brought her master to God and saved his life. How happy she must have been when she heard the news!

85

The leprosy of Naaman, captain of the host of the king of Syria, was cured when he obeyed the word of the Lord through Elisha and washed himself seven times in the Jordan.

STORY 6

Greedy Gehazi

NAAMAN was so happy and thankful that he had been cured of his leprosy that he wanted to give Elisha all the gold, silver, and beautiful garments he had brought with him.

But Elisha wanted no payment for something God had done. He hoped that this famous general would go back to his king and country and tell how the God of Israel, unlike the gods of the heathen, is willing to help the needy of all nations free of charge, "without money and without price."

"As the Lord liveth, before whom I stand," he said to Naaman, "I will receive none."

Naaman urged him, but he again refused.

Aglow with the memory of this wonderful generosity, Naaman started back for Damascus. No doubt he said to his servants, "I never saw anything like this in all my life. Imagine any man's refusing all that money I offered him! The God he serves must be different from any I ever heard about."

GREEDY GEHAZI

So the happy party moved northward, everyone in it eager to get home and tell all they had seen and heard in Israel.

Then something made Naaman look back. A man was running after them. From a distance he looked like Gehazi, Elisha's servant. What could he want?

Naaman reined in his horses, and everybody else did the same. Gehazi came up panting. Naaman got out of his chariot to greet him.

"Is all well?" he asked, a little worried.

"Oh, yes," said Gehazi cheerfully, while he made up the biggest lie of his life, "all is well. My master hath sent me, saying, Behold, even now there be come to me from mount Ephraim two young men of the sons of the prophets: give them, I pray thee, a talent of silver, and two changes of garments."

The story sounded perfectly plausible, and Naaman was most happy to oblige. "Take *two* talents," he said. "And he urged him, and bound two talents of silver in two bags, with two changes of raiment, and laid them upon two of his servants; and they bare them before him."

Naaman started up his horses again and departed, wondering whether Gehazi's story was true or whether Elisha really wanted the money for himself after all. Meanwhile Gehazi returned and hid his loot in a secret place.

But if he thought he was going to keep anything like this secret, he just didn't know his master.

"Where have you been?" asked Elisha as he entered the house again.

"Nowhere."

"Nowhere!" exclaimed the prophet in great anger. "Went not mine heart with thee, when the man turned again from his chariot to meet thee?"

Gehazi looked at the floor, ashamed. He had been found out! His awful lies were known!

But Elisha was not finished with him—yet. "Is it a time to receive money, and to receive garments, and oliveyards, and vineyards, and sheep, and oxen, and menservants, and maid-servants?" he asked sternly.

It was not; and Gehazi, as the servant of God's prophet, should have known it.

Then came his punishment: "The leprosy therefore of Naaman shall cleave unto thee, and unto thy seed for ever."

God's awful judgment on greedy Gehazi was immediately seen and "he went out from his presence a leper as white as snow."

Was the punishment too great? Not for his sin. For by his greed, selfishness, and falsehood Gehazi had spoiled something very beautiful God had tried to do for the whole kingdom of Syria and all the world beyond.

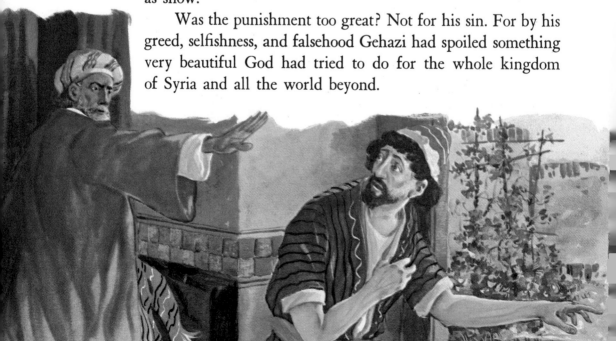

STORY 7

Elisha's Secret Army

≈≈≈≈≈≈≈≈≈≈≈≈≈≈≈≈≈≈≈≈

SOME time after Naaman's return to Damascus, the king of Syria—for some reason we do not know—declared war on Israel again.

However, something went wrong with his campaign. Every time he planned an attack or an ambush the king of Israel heard about it and prepared for it.

This happened "not once nor twice," but so many times that the king of Syria was sure he had a traitor in his camp. Sending for his officers, he said to them angrily, "Will ye not shew me which of us is for the king of Israel?"

"None, my lord, O king," replied one of the men: "but Elisha, the prophet that is in Israel, telleth the king of Israel the words that thou speakest in thy bedchamber."

It could have been Naaman himself who said this, or someone to whom he had spoken about the power of Elisha's God.

Now the problem seemed easy to the king. Get Elisha,

and all the trouble would be over. So he said to his men, "Go and spy where he is, that I may send and fetch him."

Someone said, "He is in Dothan."

So the king ordered "horses, and chariots, and a great host" to go to Dothan to fetch this man who knew too much.

Thinking to take Elisha by surprise, the army arrived by night and completely surrounded the city. There seemed no way of escape for the man of God.

Early next morning, when Elisha's servant looked from the city wall and saw all those horses and chariots, he was frightened. Running to Elisha, he cried, "Alas, my master! how shall we do?"

But Elisha wasn't troubled in the least. His trust in God was so great that nothing ever bothered him.

"Fear not," he said to the frightened young man: "for they that be with us are more than they that be with them."

The young man stared at him. How could this be? There was nobody in Dothan ready to fight these Syrians. Had Elisha some secret army?

He had. And now he prayed, saying, "Lord, I pray thee, open his eyes that he may see."

90

ELISHA'S SECRET ARMY

God answered the prayer. A moment later the young man saw what Elisha had been looking at all the time.

"Look!" he cried excitedly. "Look at them all!"

"And, behold, the mountain was full of horses and chariots of fire round about Elisha."

"And when they came down to him"—those chariots of fire he had seen once before—he knew God was very near, and he said, "Smite this people, I pray thee, with blindness."

It was a strange request, but he had a wonderful plan in mind.

Now he walked out of the city gate and bravely approached the leaders of the Syrian army, who were milling about in their blindness not knowing where they were or what to do.

"This is not the way," he said to them, "neither is this the city: follow me, and I will bring you to the man whom ye seek. But he led them to Samaria"—right into Israel's capital.

When he had them all safely inside the city gates he prayed, "Lord, open the eyes of these men, that they may see."

God did so, and the soldiers saw with sudden fear that they were in the midst of Samaria.

The king of Israel was delighted. Here was a splendid chance to teach the Syrians a lesson they would never forget. "Shall I smite them? Shall I smite them?" he said to Elisha with relish.

"No, indeed!" said Elisha. Instead, he ordered that food and water be given the prisoners, and that they be set free to go back to their homes. "And he prepared great provision for them: and when they had eaten and drunk, he sent them away, and they went to their master."

What a gracious, kindly deed that was! It was loving one's enemies in a very unusual way. And it worked, for a while at least. We read that "the bands of Syria came no more into the land of Israel."

It pays to have the protection of Elisha's secret army. You and I may have it, too. The Bible says, "The angel of the Lord encampeth round about them that fear him, and delivereth them."

STORY 8

Four Surprised Lepers

HOW many months passed before the Syrians forgot Elisha's great kindness to their soldiers, the Bible does not say. But that they did forget is certain, for the next thing we know is that Benhadad, king of Syria, marched on Samaria and surrounded it.

This time, he told himself, there would be no mistake. The Syrians would finish off Israel once and for all. So they blocked every exit and sat outside waiting for the Israelites to starve to death.

And starve they did. As weeks and months went by, the stocks of food grew lower and lower. Prices went up and up until "an ass's head" was sold for eighty pieces of silver—an enormous price. Only the rich could buy food. Hundreds of the poor died after eating refuse—and even their own children.

Never had there been such a famine. It was even worse than the one in the days of Elijah, when there was no rain for three and a half years.

Elisha lived through it all, and suffered with the people. He knew that all this distress had come as a result of the evil course followed by the king. But the king blamed *him*.

At last, when things had become about as bad as they could get, the king vowed that he would kill Elisha that very day. An executioner was sent to carry out his threat, and the king followed to make sure his command was obeyed.

"Bar the door!" Elisha ordered when he learned of the plot against his life.

Soon there was a loud knocking, but he refused to open. Then he heard the voice of the king himself. He was saying, "This trouble is from the Lord! why should I wait for the Lord any longer?"

Elisha called to him, "Hear ye the word of the Lord; . . . Tomorrow about this time shall a measure of fine flour be sold for a shekel, and two measures of barley for a shekel, in the gate of Samaria."

"Bah!" exclaimed one of the men who had come with the king. "The man must be mad! If the Lord would make windows in heaven, might this thing be?"

The prices Elisha had quoted were so low that, compared with the famine prices in the city at that time, they must have seemed silly. But though the man scoffed at him, Elisha didn't change his prophecy. Instead he said to him, "Behold, thou shalt see it with thine eyes, but shall not eat thereof."

The king and his men went away. Perhaps the king said, "We'll give him one more day, and then if nothing happens, I will surely have him put to death."

94

FOUR SURPRISED LEPERS

As usual, Elisha wasn't troubled by these angry threats. He knew that the Syrians were about to leave. His secret army —the chariots of the Lord and all their shining hosts—were about to move into action once more, and there was nothing to fear.

That very evening, in His own wonderful way, the Lord "made the host of the Syrians to hear a noise of chariots, and a noise of horses, even the noise of a great host: and they said one to another, Lo, the king of Israel hath hired against us the kings of the Hittites, and the kings of the Egyptians, to come upon us. Wherefore they arose and fled in the twilight, and left their tents, and their horses, and their asses, even the camp as it was, and fled for their life."

The first to discover that the Syrian hosts had gone were four lepers who had been slowly dying of hunger outside the gate of Samaria. It so happened that this very day they had said

to one another, "We're going to die anyway; let's go to the Syrians and see if they will give us something to eat."

So as twilight fell they walked over to the Syrian camp and found nobody there. They couldn't believe their eyes. They thought there must be some mistake.

Going from tent to tent, they found the Syrians had left all their valuables behind—money, clothes, all sorts of things, and, best of all, food! Heaps and piles of food! What a find! And what a feed! They stuffed themselves with the best of everything. Then they gathered up silver and gold and garments of all kinds, and hid them.

By and by their consciences began to trouble them. They felt a bit selfish, enjoying themselves so much while so many people were starving to death inside the city. So they made their way in the dark to the city gate, called the sleepy porter, and told him their amazing story. He called the other porters, and though it was late at night, they sent word to the king.

He was in bed asleep when the news reached him. When awakened he didn't know whether to believe it or not. He was sure that, even if it was true, it was only a trap the Syrians had set. They were no doubt waiting in the mountains for the Israelites to come out; then they would pounce upon them.

FOUR SURPRISED LEPERS

Somebody suggested that five horsemen be sent out to look things over. This seemed a good idea, but they couldn't find five horses able to go. So they sent two.

These scouts followed the trail of the Syrians clear to the Jordan. All the way they found "garments and vessels, which the Syrians had cast away in their haste."

When they got back to Samaria word spread like wildfire about the empty camp. Soon the poor, starving people were pouring out of the city gates in thousands. They found so much food that there was enough to stock the shops again. Prices dropped so low that a measure of fine flour was sold for a shekel and two measures of barley for a shekel, just as Elisha had said.

As for the man who had laughed at Elisha's prophecy, the king put him in charge of the city gate to care for the heavy traffic. But so great was the crush that he was knocked down, trampled on, and killed. So he saw the cheap food— for everybody was carrying some of it—but he never had a chance to eat any. It never pays to make fun of a prophet of the Lord.

STORY 9

Making Iron Float

MANY were the miracles God wrought through His faithful servant Elisha. Perhaps it was because the times were so dark, and His people were so poor and needy, that He revealed His power in so many wonderful ways.

Once when Elisha was visiting the school of the prophets at Gilgal he found that the students had very little to eat. Seeing how hungry the young men were, he said, "Set on the great pot!" and everybody began to look forward to a good meal.

While the food was cooking, one of the students, anxious to help, brought a heap of wild gourds and shredded them into the pot, not knowing that they were poisonous.

When mealtime came the young people sat around licking their lips. With Elisha in charge they knew they would fare well. Eagerly they watched as the food was poured from the pot.

MAKING IRON FLOAT

Then came a bitter disappointment. Somebody recognized the taste of the wild gourds.

"Don't eat!" he cried. "There is death in the pot."

Poor, hungry students! All looked at Elisha, shocked that he should have let them down like this.

But he hadn't. Nor was he upset.

"Bring meal," he said, and they brought some. Then he cast it into the pot.

"Now start pouring again," he said.

They did, and, lo, the bitter taste had gone and the poison had vanished.

Another time when he was meeting with a group of people—about a hundred altogether—somebody brought him twenty barley loaves and some ears of grain in a sack.

"Give them unto the people, that they may eat," he said.

"What, should I set this before an hundred men?" his servant asked.

"Yes," said Elisha. "Give the people, that they may eat: for thus saith the Lord, They shall eat, and shall leave thereof."

It was just like the miracle of the loaves and fishes which Jesus wrought more than eight hundred years later. There was plenty for everyone and lots left over.

One day the leaders of one of the schools of the prophets came to Elisha and reported that their buildings were over-crowded. There was no room for all the young people who wanted to attend. So would it be all right to put up a new building? They would cut the trees and do the rest of the work themselves to keep expenses down.

Elisha said the plan sounded good to him, and he wished them well.

100

MAKING IRON FLOAT

"Come with us," they urged, anxious for his good advice.

"I will go," he said, and went with them.

Arriving at the Jordan, they all began cutting down trees along the riverbank.

Suddenly there was a cry of alarm.

"My ax!" cried one of the students. "The head has fallen off in the water! Alas, master! for it was borrowed!"

"Where did it fall?" asked Elisha.

"Over there," said the young man, pointing to the place where it had disappeared.

Elisha cut a stick and threw it toward the spot, while everybody looked to see what would happen.

Suddenly the axhead floated to the surface as though it had been made of wood.

"Pick it up," said Elisha as he walked away.

The boy did so, his heart bursting with gratitude to his master and his God.

STORY 10

Arrows of Deliverance

GRADUALLY the years slipped by. Elisha moved from palaces to hovels, talking freely with kings and common people. Some loved him, others hated him. In a time of war, famine, and much suffering he was like a tower of strength to all who remained loyal to the God of heaven.

Then he fell sick with "the sickness whereof he died."

While he was on his deathbed, Joash, king of Israel, came to visit him. With tears the king cried, "O my father, my father, the chariot of Israel, and the horsemen thereof!" It was his way of saying how much the old prophet meant to him and his kingdom. And his words meant still more in view of the fact that he had just lost all but ten of his chariots to the king of Syria.

Elisha knew how discouraged the king was, so he said, "Take bow and arrows."

The king did so.

"Put your hand upon the bow," said the old man.

102

ARROWS OF DELIVERANCE

The king obeyed, and Elisha put his hands upon the king's hands, to let him know that God would be with him.

"Open the window eastward," said Elisha.

Again the king did as he was asked.

"Shoot!" said Elisha. And he shot.

"The arrow of the Lord's deliverance!" cried the prophet as the feathered shaft sped toward the rising sun; "and the arrow of deliverance from Syria: for you shall smite the Syrians in Aphek, till you have consumed them."

Then he said to the king, "Take the arrows."

The king took them.

"Smite upon the ground," said Elisha.

The king banged the arrows on the ground three times.

"No!" cried the prophet heatedly. "You should have hit them five or six times; then you would have smitten Syria till you had consumed it."

Even the striking of the arrows on the ground meant more than the king understood. He should have banged those arrows down five, six, seven, ten times, to show his eagerness to do the work God wanted him to do.

After this Elisha became weaker and weaker, and he knew his end was near. Perhaps he wondered sometimes whether the fiery chariot that had taken Elijah to heaven would come for him. But no chariot came. So he died as others die, "and they buried him."

Someday, however, in the glorious morning of the resurrection, he will awake to see that chariot after all, coming straight toward him, with the shining horsemen of heaven eager to carry him home.

PART III

Stories of Conflict and Blessing

(2 KINGS 13:21-16:20; 2 CHRONICLES 17:1-31:21)

STORY 1

The Choir That Won a Battle

ONE DOES not often hear of an army's being led into battle by a choir, but that is what happened when Jehoshaphat was king of Judah.

One day a messenger arrived in Jerusalem with news that the Moabites and Ammonites were on their way with thousands of soldiers to attack the city.

Knowing the weakness of his own forces, Jehoshaphat turned to God for help. He also sent word to all the cities of Judah urging the people to come to the Temple and pray.

Soon fathers and mothers, boys and girls, began streaming into the city from all directions, packing the court of the house of the Lord. It must have been a marvelous sight, for so many people were there that it seemed as though "all Judah" was standing humbly before the Lord with "their little ones, their wives, and their children."

By and by good king Jehoshaphat began to pray. Such a beautiful prayer it was, too!

107

As the enemy came near, the Lord gave Jahaziel a message for the people, "Be not afraid nor dismayed by reason of this great multitude; for the battle is not your's, but God's."

"O Lord God of our fathers," he cried, "art thou not God in heaven? and rulest not thou over all the kingdoms of the heathen? and in thine hand is there not power and might, so that none is able to withstand thee?

"Art not thou our God, who didst drive out the inhabitants of this land before thy people Israel, and gavest it to the seed of Abraham thy friend for ever?"

He went on to remind God of Solomon's prayer at the dedication of the Temple: "If, when evil cometh upon us, as the sword, judgment, or pestilence, or famine, we stand before this house, and in thy presence, . . . and cry unto thee in our affliction, then thou wilt hear and help."

Then he told of the approach of the Moabites and the Ammonites, saying, "O our God, wilt *thou* not judge them? for *we* have no might against this great company that cometh against us; neither know we what to do: but our eyes are upon thee."

Scarcely had the king ended his prayer when another voice was heard. All eyes turned to see who was speaking. It was young Jahaziel, a Levite, and it was clear that God had given him a message to cheer the people in this dark hour.

"Thus saith the Lord unto you," he cried aloud, so that the whole great congregation could hear him. "Be not afraid nor dismayed by reason of this great multitude; for the battle is not your's, but God's."

THE CHOIR THAT WON A BATTLE

What a sigh of relief went up! God was going to help them! He had taken over the problem and was going to solve it in His own way!

"Ye shall not need to fight in this battle," the young Levite continued. "Set yourselves, stand ye still, and see the salvation of the Lord with you . . . : fear not, nor be dismayed; tomorrow go out against them: for the Lord will be with you."

As Jahaziel finished speaking, king and people bowed humbly before God, thanking Him for His gracious promise of deliverance.

Nobody doubted that God would do as His prophet had said. Boldly Jehoshaphat declared, "Believe in the Lord your God, so shall ye be established; believe his prophets, so shall ye prosper."

Early next morning all was bustle and excitement as the troops prepared to leave. Jehoshaphat moved among them speaking words of encouragement. As he did so somebody had a bright idea. Just who it was we are not told, but the man suggested to the king that if God was going to win a great victory this day, why not thank Him for it in advance? Why not let the temple choir go ahead and lead the whole army in songs of praise?

The king thought this was a fine suggestion. At once

he "appointed singers unto the Lord, . . . that should praise the beauty of holiness."

So for the first time in history a choir went out to battle ahead of the soldiers. No doubt all the rest joined in, singing as they marched, "Praise the Lord; for his mercy endureth for ever."

What a scene to remember! Surely all who looked down from the city walls on that long column of singing men, and heard their deep bass voices echoing back from the mountains, must have felt that this was one of the greatest moments in Jerusalem's history.

And what happened?

The Bible says that "when they began to sing and to praise, the Lord set ambushments" against the Ammonites and the Moabites, "and they were smitten."

Exactly what took place we do not know, but it seems that of a sudden the enemy soldiers began to quarrel among themselves. In the fighting that followed, thousands were killed, and when Jehoshaphat's singing army arrived on the scene they found only dead bodies. They didn't have to fight at all, just as God had said through Jahaziel.

For three days they walked among the dead, gathering the spoil, "both riches . . . and precious jewels . . . more than they could carry away. And on the fourth day they assembled themselves in the valley of Berachah [or blessing]; for there they blessed the Lord."

So they sang their way to victory. And because they trusted God the valley of fear became the valley of blessing.

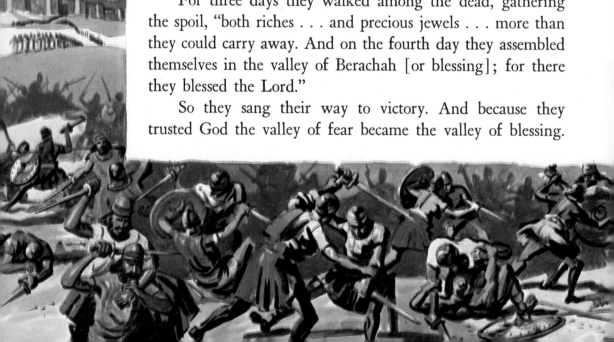

STORY 2

Baby Hid in the Temple

W HEN good king Jehoshaphat died much trouble came to the kingdom of Judah, even as it had come already to the northern kingdom of Israel. Jehoram, the new king, was very different from his father. He had married Athaliah, a daughter of the wicked king Ahab, and she had turned his heart from God to Baal.

The first thing he did on ascending the throne was to kill all his brothers—such a dreadful thing to do! Then he went on to walk "in the way of the kings of Israel."

Because of his sins God left him to face his enemies alone. When the Philistines and the Arabians came up to attack Jerusalem, no divine "ambushments" were set against them, nor did any chariots of fire come to the rescue. Instead, the enemy soldiers broke into the city, raided the king's house, and took captive his wives and all his sons save Ahaziah, the youngest. Soon after that Jehoram himself died of a very painful disease, having reigned but eight years.

111

Ahaziah took his father's place on the throne and reigned only one year. His mother Athaliah "was his counsellor to do wickedly," so that he did "evil in the sight of the Lord like the house of Ahab." When his uncle, the king of Israel, asked him to go to war against the Syrians, he did so, only to be killed in the fighting.

Now a strange and terrible thing happened. When news of her son's death reached Athaliah, she set out to kill all his children—her own grandchildren!—no doubt thinking that if there was nobody else to take the throne, she would be queen.

She almost succeeded in her wicked scheme, and would have done so but for the presence of mind of the children's aunt, Jehoshabeath. Hearing of the sad fate of her nephews and nieces, this good woman—whose long name means that she had vowed to serve Jehovah—grabbed little two-year-old Joash and rushed him to the Temple buildings. Being the high priest's wife, she knew the place well, and putting the boy and his nurse in an out-of-the-way bedroom, locked them in. She guessed that nobody would be likely to find them there, and nobody did.

P. Remney

BABY HID IN THE TEMPLE

So it was that little Joash, like Samuel of old, grew up in the Temple. Nearly six years he lived there, being trained in the ways of truth and right by his aunt and uncle.

Meanwhile the wicked Athaliah, thinking that all "the seed royal" were dead, ruled as she pleased, trying to get the people of Jerusalem to worship Baal as did the Israelites in Samaria.

Fortunately Jehoiada the high priest was a true servant of the God of heaven. He hated all the evil the queen was doing. And he knew, better than anyone else, that she had no right to the throne. Quietly he gathered his friends around him, telling them in secret that the true heir was still alive.

I doubt whether he told anybody just where the boy was hidden, lest the secret get to the ears of the queen. But he told enough so that none doubted the truth of his words.

Gradually the spirit of revolt spread. As years passed, more and more people made up their minds to get rid of the usurper and put the rightful king on the throne.

At last the plot was ready. Jehoiada called the leading conspirators to meet him in the Temple. Then, when all were present, he brought out little Joash, now seven years old, for them to see. How they cheered and cheered! Jehoiada now put a crown on the boy's head, while everybody shouted, "God save the king! God save the king!"

Hearing the noise, Queen Athaliah hurried over to the Temple to find out what it was all about. To her amazement the place was filled with people singing and shouting for joy, led by trumpeters and the Temple choir.

Suddenly she caught sight of the little boy king, wearing a crown and royal robes. Who could this be? she wondered. Had she not killed all her grandsons—everybody who might have had a claim to the throne?

"Treason! Treason!" she screamed.

But no one came to her aid. Instead, some of Jehoiada's men carried her out of the Temple and put her to death.

With the wicked usurper out of the way, a great procession was formed, and young King Joash was led in triumph to the king's house and placed upon "the throne of the kingdom."

He must have looked very small and frightened in that big chair, but everybody was glad to see him there. "And all the people of the land rejoiced: and the city was quiet" again.

STORY 3

Boy With a Money Box

HAVING been brought up in the Temple by Jehoiada and his good wife Jehoshabeath, it was natural that Joash should serve the God of heaven. It was also natural that he should want to repair the Temple, where he had spent most of his boyhood years.

He had many reasons for being thankful to God and to the priests who had watched over him so long at great risk to their lives. No doubt, too, Jehoiada had more than once suggested to him that he might show his gratitude by restoring the house of God.

It surely needed fixing. Though less than two hundred years had passed since its dedication, it was a wreck compared with what it had been in King Solomon's day. Not only had it been raided by the soldiers of Pharaoh Shishak and the Philistines and Arabians, but the sons of Queen Athaliah had "broken up the house of God" and taken all the "dedicated things" and put them in the temple of Baal.

115

Soon after he was made king, Joash called the priests and Levites together and ordered them to go to all the cities of Judah and gather money to repair the Temple. "And be quick about it," he told them, anxious that the work should be started as soon as possible.

The Levites, however, did not hurry themselves. Perhaps they said to one another, "The king's still a boy, so why should we take any notice of him?"

When the king learned that his command had been disobeyed, and that money was only trickling in, he sent for Jehoiada and asked him what was the matter with the Levites and why they were so slack in their duties.

He wanted more speed, more action. Then, just like a boy, he suggested a very simple way to get the money quickly. What about putting a big box, or chest, outside the Temple gate and asking everybody to put something in it?

Jehoiada agreed that the idea was worth trying and so, "at the king's commandment they made a chest, and set it without at the gate of the house of the Lord."

The Bible doesn't say so, but I feel sure that King Joash was the first to put an offering into that box, as a worthy example to his people.

Right after him came the princes of the realm and all the merchants of the city, each dropping in some gift. As word about the king's money box spread through the country, people came flocking to Jerusalem by the thousands to see it. This was

something new and different and the boy king's own idea.

Soon there was a long line of men and women, boys and girls, waiting to put something in the box. Every moment the chink of gold or silver could be heard. The children loved it.

By and by a servant ran to the king with news that the box was full. It wouldn't hold another shekel. Joash could hardly believe his ears. He ordered that the box be brought to him and opened in his presence.

As "the king's scribe and the high priest's officer" tipped up the box in "the king's office," and poured out piles of gold and silver, the young king was delighted. Probably he had never seen so much money before, for the priests of the Lord had been very poor during the reign of Queen Athaliah, when he was hidden in the Temple.

"Let it be filled again!" he said, and the empty box was put in its place outside the Temple, where more people were eagerly waiting to put money into it.

By nightfall the box was full once more. Again it was emptied before the king, who was overjoyed at the success of his plan.

"Thus they did day by day, and gathered money in abundance."

As the silver and gold came in it was used to hire "masons and carpenters . . . , also such as wrought iron and brass to mend the house of the Lord."

How long it took to make all the repairs we are not told, but at last the work was done. When all the bills were paid it was found that there was still much money left over. This was used to make vessels of gold and silver for the priests to use in the Temple services.

What happened to the money box nobody knows, but it served its purpose; and the story of it lets us see how even a little boy can have a very bright idea.

STORY 4

The King Who Became a Leper

SAD TO say, the boy with the money box did not keep true to God all his life. It doesn't seem possible, but after the death of the high priest Jehoiada (at 130 years of age) some of the princes persuaded Joash to begin worshiping idols. Worse still, when Jehoiada's son Zechariah told him how wrong this was, Joash killed him.

After all the kindness Jehoiada had shown him, this was the meanest thing the king could have done. God was very displeased with him.

Punishment soon came. A band of Syrians attacked Jerusalem, sacked the city, killed the princes, and left Joash himself badly wounded.

Seeing Joash helpless in bed, two of his servants murdered him in revenge for the killing of Zechariah. Such was the sad end of a boy who started well but lost his way and followed wicked men to do evil.

Amaziah took his place on the throne. He, too, started

out well, and God gave him victories over his enemies. But— of all things!—he brought back his defeated enemies' idols and worshiped them! Said a prophet of the Lord to him, "Why hast thou sought after the gods of the people, which could not deliver their own people out of thine hand?"

Because of Amaziah's folly God allowed great trouble to come upon him. The king of Israel came from the north, broke down a large part of the wall of Jerusalem, and took away all the gold and silver out of the Temple.

Thus all the money the people had so gladly dropped into Joash's money box some years before was lost. What a pity! What a price there is to pay for sin!

Sad, too, was the end of Amaziah, for his people rose against him, chased him as far as Lachish, and killed him. Then they brought his body on horseback to Jerusalem for burial.

Taking Amaziah's place on the throne was a fine young man of sixteen named Uzziah. His mother, Jecoliah, was a very good woman, who had brought him up to love God. So "he did that which was right in the sight of the Lord."

Uzziah's reign was one of the longest in history—fifty-two years—and "as long as he sought the Lord, God made him to prosper."

And how God did make Uzziah prosper! He subdued the Philistines and won victories over many other nations, extending his power to the border of Egypt.

He built up his army until he had over three hundred thousand men fitted out with the very latest weapons, including engines to "shoot arrows and great stones withal."

120

He fortified Jerusalem by building new towers on the walls. "In the low country, and in the plains" he built many strong points to protect his wells, vineyards, and cattle against his enemies.

The Bible says that "he was marvellously helped, till he was strong." Then came the "but" in his life.

"But when he was strong, his heart was lifted up to his destruction." In other words, when he was strong he grew proud, and this destroyed him.

All of us face the same danger. How often when we receive great blessings from God, we think we won them by our own efforts! And the moment we do so we ask for trouble, for "pride goeth before a fall."

Because of all the success God had given him, Uzziah thought he could go into the Temple and burn incense like the priests. Why not? In what way were they better than he?

When the high priest heard what the king had done, he

121

"went in after him" into the Temple, with eighty priests behind him.

Uzziah was standing by the altar of incense, swinging a censer.

Boldly the high priest said to the king, "It is not for you, Uzziah, to burn incense to the Lord, but for the priests, the sons of Aaron, who are consecrated to burn incense. Go out of the sanctuary; for you have done wrong, and it will bring you no honour from the Lord God."

At this the king lost his temper. How dare anyone question his right to go where he pleased in his kingdom—even into the Temple itself? Was the high priest more holy than he?

But even as he stormed at the priests, a white spot appeared on his forehead. The priests recognized it at once, and a gasp of horror rose from them.

"Leprosy! Leprosy!" they cried.

As the awful truth dawned upon the king he hurried out of the Temple, the priests following. He knew that he had been smitten as a judgment from God, and his pride quickly ebbed away.

King Uzziah was a leper the rest of his life. He had to live alone in a separate house and never again was he permitted to enter the Temple.

He could have been "marvellously helped" all his days. He could have prospered in his latter years as when he sought the Lord in his youth. What a pity he made that one mistake! What a pity he let foolish pride spoil everything!

STORY 5

Captives Set Free

AFTER Uzziah's death his son Jotham came to the throne and reigned sixteen years. He was followed by Ahaz, a very wicked man, who not only made molten images to Baal but "cut in pieces the vessels of the house of God," shut the Temple doors, and made altars "in every corner of Jerusalem." Worse still, he even "burnt his children in the fire, after the abominations of the heathen."

Because of his dreadful sins great punishment came upon him. Soon he lost all that his grandfather Uzziah had built up in the days when God prospered him.

Judah was invaded by the Syrians, Edomites, and Philistines, all of whom carried away many captives and much spoil. Then the Israelites swept through the land and took a host of prisoners to Samaria.

There must have been many broken homes and broken hearts in Judah after these many attacks. How poor, how wretched, everybody who was left must have felt!

Of the invasion by the Israelites the Bible says: "And the children of Israel carried away captive of their brethren two hundred thousand, women, sons, and daughters . . . to Samaria."

Imagine it! What a scene of misery! The wounded men, the frightened women, the sobbing boys and girls. What moans of anguish! What prayers for help!

The heart of God was touched by the tragic sight. This was too much. Punishment had gone far enough. Before the sad procession reached Samaria He had already sent someone to deliver them.

"A prophet of the Lord was *there,* whose name was Oded." "There," where help was most needed.

This brave man went out to meet the soldiers who were bringing the great host of prisoners to Samaria. As he saw the long, long line of men, women, and children, many tied together with ropes, others with feet cut and bleeding, all weak and weary after their long, forced march from Judea, his eyes glowed with anger.

Sternly he rebuked the soldiers, in words like these: "Because God was angry with Judah He delivered them into your hand, and you have slain them in a rage; now you propose to keep the children of Judah for bondmen and bondwomen: but are there not with you, even with you, sins against the Lord God?"

Then he commanded that the prisoners be released.

"Hear me therefore," he cried earnestly, "and deliver the captives . . . : for the fierce wrath of the Lord is upon you!"

The procession stopped. Prisoners who had heard the

prophet's words took new hope. Word spread down the line that God had sent help. Their prayers were about to be answered. Bowed heads were raised; tears were dried. Many a boy and girl looked up and said, "I told you so, Mamma; I knew God wouldn't forget us."

Meanwhile the leaders of the soldiers argued back and forth. Some said, "Why should we listen to this fellow? We're not going to give up our prisoners. Think of the trouble it cost us to get them!"

Then four very noble men spoke up. Their names were Azariah, Berechiah, Jehizkiah, and Amasa, and they deserve to be remembered among the great men of history.

These four were among the thousands of people who had come hurrying out of Samaria to meet the returning soldiers. They did not like what they saw. They agreed with the prophet Oded and took their stand with him. Indeed, they went further. Very firmly they said to the soldiers, "You shall not bring the captives in here, for you propose to bring upon us guilt against the Lord in addition to our present sins and guilt. For our guilt is already great, and there is fierce wrath against Israel."

Ashamed of what they had done, the soldiers slunk away, leaving the captives and the spoil.

Then these four noble men, Azariah, Berechiah, Jehizkiah, and Amasa, did one of the finest things mentioned in the Bible. They took all the poor captives and with the spoil (made up largely of garments, as well as money) "clothed all that were naked among them" and "gave them sandals, provided them with food and drink, and anointed them; and carrying all that were feeble among them on asses, they brought them to their kinsfolk at Jericho, the city of palm trees. Then they returned to Samaria."

What a different procession it must have been going the other way—back home again! All fears gone, all tears dried all eyes bright with thankfulness and new hope! How the boys and girls must have shouted for joy as they hopped and skipped about on that glorious homeward journey!

And how pleased God must have been with that most gracious deed of the four noble men! If only there had been more men like them in Israel, the kingdom might have stood forever.

STORY 6

Two Wonderful Weeks

D O YOU remember Jehoiada—the high priest who cared for little Joash in the Temple? And do you remember how he had a son named Zechariah, who was later killed by that very same Joash? Well, this Zechariah had a little girl called Abijah who grew up to be one of the most important women in the Bible.

You see, Abijah, who loved the Lord, became the wife of King Ahaz and had a son whom she called Hezekiah. While her wicked husband was trying to make the people of Judah turn to Baal, she was quietly bringing up her precious baby to love and honor the God of heaven.

What Abijah had to put up with we shall never know, but through it all she kept true to the faith of her father and grandfather. And so when Ahaz died, she had a son ready to sit on the throne who hated all the evil that his father had done.

Hezekiah was twenty-five years old when he began to

127

reign, and, thanks to his mother's careful training, "he did that which was right in the sight of the Lord."

His very first act after his coronation was to open the doors of the Temple which his father had closed. Then he ordered the Levites to go in and clean out all the dirt that had gathered while the place had been shut, and to start the services again.

Before the work began he called the priests and Levites together in East Street and talked with them. After bidding them sanctify *themselves* before starting to cleanse the *Temple,* he went on to say, "Our fathers have . . . done that which was evil in the eyes of the Lord our God. . . . They have shut up the doors of the porch, and put out the lamps, and have not burned incense nor offered burnt offerings. . . .

"Wherefore the wrath of the Lord was upon Judah and Jerusalem, and he hath delivered them to trouble, . . . as ye see with your own eyes. For lo, our fathers have fallen by the sword, and our sons and our daughters and our wives are in captivity for this.

"Now it is in mine heart to make a covenant with the Lord God of Israel, that his fierce wrath may turn away from us.

"My sons, be not now negligent: for the Lord hath chosen you to stand before him, to serve him."

Thus encouraged by the king, everybody went to work with a will. And how they did put their hearts into it!

"The priests went into the inner parts of the house of the Lord, to cleanse it, and brought out all the uncleanness

5-9

— PAINTING BY HERBERT RUDEEN   © 1955, BY REVIEW AND HERALD

Due to his good mother's careful training, the first act of the young King Hezekiah after his coronation was to open the doors of the Temple which his father years before had closed.

that they found . . . into the court." Then the Levites carried the rubbish out of the city and tipped it into the brook Kidron.

It took a whole week to get the worst of the job done, and another week to finish it properly. Then both priests and Levites went to King Hezekiah to report.

"We have cleansed all the house of the Lord," they said, "and the altar of burnt offering, with all the vessels thereof, and the shewbread table. . . . Moreover all the vessels, which King Ahaz in his reign did cast away in his transgression, have we prepared and sanctified, and, behold, they are before the altar of the Lord."

Hezekiah was surprised that they had finished so soon, and very, very pleased. The next morning he rose early and, taking all the rulers of the city with him, went to the Temple. As a sacrifice he brought seven bullocks, seven rams, seven lambs, seven he-goats, and "commanded the priests the sons of Aaron to offer them on the altar of the Lord." This was a sin-offering for all Israel.

130

TWO WONDERFUL WEEKS

As soon as the fire was kindled and the smoke of the sacrifice began to rise into the early morning air, there was a burst of song and music. Priests blew the sacred trumpets while Levites played on cymbals, psalteries, and harps as they sang "the song of the Lord."

Everybody was happy that the Temple was open again and that from now on the worship of God would be continued as of old. "And they sang praises with gladness, and they bowed their heads and worshipped."

It was a great day. After the sin offering was consumed Hezekiah called upon the people to bring thank offerings, which they did with cheerful hearts. Six hundred oxen and three thousand sheep were brought—so many that the priests were too few to handle them, and "their brethren the Levites" had to help them.

It must have been a wonderful sight with so many people eagerly bringing their gifts. Jerusalem hadn't seen anything like this for many a long day.

"And Hezekiah rejoiced, and all the people, that God had prepared the people: for the thing was done suddenly."

"Suddenly" was the word. Little more than two weeks had passed since the doors of the Temple had been unlocked and the work of cleaning up begun.

Some people had thought it might take months, maybe years, before the place could be fixed up properly so the worship of God could be started again. But it had happened in just two weeks—two wonderful weeks!

It seemed too good to be true. Yet it was true. The Temple was open. Worship had begun. The smoke of the sacrifices was even now billowing heavenward. No wonder Hezekiah was happy! So was his mother, Abijah. For her it was a dream come true. This was her moment of triumph after all the dark years she had lived with wicked Ahaz. How her father and her grandfather would have rejoiced to see this day!

It just goes to show how quickly a task can be done when people have a mind to do it. It doesn't have to wait and wait and wait. When there are willing hearts, and a desire to serve, the thing can be done "suddenly."

STORY 7

Great Joy in Jerusalem

CHEERED by what happened when the Temple was opened again, King Hezekiah suggested to his counselors that it would be a fine thing if the whole nation —Israel as well as Judah—would celebrate the Passover as in the days of old.

It was a bold idea, for only a few years had passed since soldiers from Samaria had taken away those two hundred thousand captives we read about. Fancy proposing to throw open the gates of Jerusalem to people who could be so cruel!

But the king was so sure he was right, and that God would bless the plan, that he persuaded everybody to agree to it.

Then he sent messengers all over Palestine, from "Beersheba even to Dan," inviting the people to come "to keep the passover unto the Lord God of Israel at Jerusalem."

"So the posts went with the letters from the king and his princes throughout all Israel and Judah."

133

"Ye children of Israel," ran the message, "turn again unto the Lord God of Abraham, Isaac, and Israel, and he will return to . . . you. . . . Yield yourselves unto the Lord, and enter into his sanctuary, . . . and serve the Lord your God. . . . For if ye turn again unto the Lord, your brethren and your children shall find compassion before them that lead them captive, so that they shall come again into this land: for the Lord your God is gracious and merciful, and will not turn away his face from you, if ye return unto him."

It was a very beautiful message and much more important than anybody—even Hezekiah himself—understood at the moment. In fact, it was Israel's last chance, their last hope of escape from the doom that was now so near them.

Already the Assyrians had invaded northern Palestine and taken away many captives. Soon—very soon—the same enemy would return and carry off almost the whole population. Had the people of Israel accepted Hezekiah's invitation, and turned from their sins, God would have saved them as He saved Jerusalem. But they did not accept it.

GREAT JOY IN JERUSALEM

As Hezekiah's messengers "passed from city to city," the people "laughed them to scorn, and mocked them." Some thought it was a trick. Others said it was foolish trying to get so many people to travel to Jerusalem in such dangerous times. "What's the use?" asked others. "Why revive the old Passover service now?"

A few accepted the invitation, but in general the response from Israel was not good. In Judah, however, the people had "one heart to do the commandment of the king." They came to Jerusalem by thousands, and "there assembled . . . much people to keep the feast . . . a very great congregation."

When everybody had arrived it was decided first to cleanse Jerusalem of every trace of idol worship. So the people broke down all the altars that had been built in honor of heathen gods and threw them into the brook Kidron.

Then the service of the Passover began. Because of the crowds many of those who had come from a distance had not been able to wash themselves as they were supposed to do before taking part in this very solemn service; but when Hezekiah heard of it, he "prayed for them, saying, The good Lord pardon every one that prepareth his heart to seek God, the Lord God of his fathers, though he be not cleansed according to the purification of the sanctuary."

That prayer showed what a great man Hezekiah was. He believed God cares more about what goes on inside a person's heart than how clean his hands or feet may be. And he was right. The Bible says the Lord heard Hezekiah "and healed the people."

What a glorious time they had together! For seven days they kept the feast "with great gladness: and the Levites and the priests praised the Lord day by day, singing with loud instruments unto the Lord."

Everybody enjoyed themselves so much that it was decided to keep the feast another seven days. And the second week was as happy as the first.

"And all the congregation of Judah, . . . and all the congregation that came out of Israel, and the strangers that came out of the land of Israel, and that dwelt in Judah, rejoiced. So there was great joy in Jerusalem: for since the time of Solomon the son of David king of Israel there was not the like in Jerusalem."

STORY 8

Heaps and Heaps of Blessings

FILLED with joy over the turn events had taken, the people streamed out of Jerusalem with their minds made up to put an end to idol worship once and for all. They went through all the cities of Judah breaking images to pieces and smashing altars "until they had utterly destroyed them all."

This done, Hezekiah suggested that the people start paying tithe again for the support of the priests and Levites and the work of the house of God.

Gladly they agreed to do so. All were so happy about the wonderful reformation taking place that as soon as the king's wishes were known "the children of Israel brought in abundance the firstfruits of corn, wine, and oil, and honey, and of all the increase of the field; and the tithe of all things brought they in abundantly."

Besides all this they "brought in the tithe of oxen and sheep, and the tithe of holy things which were consecrated unto the Lord their God, and laid them by heaps."

137

Never had anything like this been seen before—at least, not since the days of Solomon. Right from the start there was too much for the regular places of storage. "In the third month they began to lay the foundation of the heaps, and finished them in the seventh." In other words, for four months the people kept bringing their tithes and gifts until at last there were heaps and heaps and heaps, all over the place.

Hearing what had happened, the king went to see for himself. "And when Hezekiah and the princes came and saw the heaps, they blessed the Lord, and his people Israel."

The priests blessed the people, too, for this was the first time in years that they had had enough to eat. "This great store," said Azariah, the chief priest, to the king, "is that which is left" after the priests and Levites had eaten to the full.

As for the dear people, they did not lose by their generosity. No, indeed. While they gave heaps and heaps of their good things to God, He gave them heaps and heaps of blessings in return.

Now the question arose as to what should be done with all that the people had brought in.

Ever practical, Hezekiah gave orders that storehouses should be built within the Temple grounds. This was done, and the Levites "brought in the offerings and the tithes and the dedicated things faithfully."

There was so much stuff of all kinds that Hezekiah appointed a committee of twelve men to look after it, with Cononiah as chairman.

As the years passed it seemed as if everything that King Hezekiah started was a success. No doubt it was because he "wrought that which was good and right and truth before the Lord his God. And in every work that he began in the service of the house of God, and in the law, and in the commandments, to seek his God, he did it with all his heart, and prospered."

That sort of program will spell success for anybody.

PART IV

Stories of Kings and Prophets

(2 KINGS 17:1-25:30; 2 CHRONICLES 32:1-36:21)

STORY 1

Why Israel Fell

I
T WAS just a little while—a few short years—after that
wonderful Passover in Jerusalem that Samaria fell to the
Assyrians and the kingdom of Israel came to an end.

Hoshea was on the throne—the last of the kings of Israel.
Like all who had reigned before him, "he did that which was
evil in the sight of the Lord."

Shalmaneser, king of Assyria, had asked Hoshea for a very
large sum of money. Unable to pay it, he had turned for
help, not to God, but to King So of Egypt. This was a big
mistake, for not only was King So unable to help him, but
when King Shalmaneser heard what he had done he was
furious.

Marching on Samaria with a huge army, he surrounded
the city. The siege lasted three years, and many of the people
inside died of starvation. This time there was no Elisha to come
to the rescue, nor did any chariots of the Lord draw near to
frighten away the invaders.

143

When Hoshea, king of Israel, turned to Baal
instead of to the true God for help in the siege
of Samaria, the Assyrians broke down the
gates and drove all the people into captivity.

No doubt Hoshea and his people cried to Baal to deliver them, but no help came. It was the final proof to the people of Israel how worthless were all the idols they had worshiped.

At last everybody was too feeble to resist any longer. The gates of the city were broken open, and the Assyrian soldiers rushed in. Many people were put to death and the rest were carried away into captivity.

The same thing happened in every city and village of Israel, for "the king of Assyria came up throughout all the land, . . . and carried Israel away into Assyria, and placed them in Halah and in Habor by the river of Gozan, and in the cities of the Medes."

It was a sad, sad ending to what could have been a glorious history.

In little more than two hundred years Israel had fallen from its place among the greatest and richest nations on earth to a scattered group of wretched, poverty-stricken captives.

In just two hundred years they had lost everything—their land, their homes, their furniture, their cattle, their money,

their honor. They had nothing left of all that God had given them. And why?

Because they turned away from the God of heaven. From Jeroboam to Hoshea just twenty kings sat on the throne of Israel, and every one of them was a rebel against God. Every one of them worshiped Baal and led the people into evil.

"For so it was, that the children of Israel had sinned against the Lord their God, which had brought them up out of the land of Egypt, . . . and walked in the statutes of the heathen, whom the Lord cast out from before the children of Israel. . . .

"And the children of Israel did secretly those things that were not right against the Lord their God. . . .

"And they set them up images and groves in every high hill, and under every green tree: and there they burnt incense in all the high places, as did the heathen whom the Lord carried away before them; and wrought wicked things to provoke the Lord to anger: for they served idols, whereof the Lord had said unto them, Ye shall not do this thing."

Time and again God had pleaded with them to turn from their wickedness. He had sent Elijah, Elisha, and other prophets to them saying, "Turn ye from your evil ways, and keep my commandments and my statutes," but they had "hardened their necks, like to the neck of their fathers, that they did not believe in the Lord their God.

"And they left all the commandments of the Lord their God, and made them molten images, even two calves, and made a grove, and worshipped all the host of heaven, and served Baal.

"And they caused their sons and their daughters to pass through the fire, and used divination and enchantments, and sold themselves to do evil in the sight of the Lord, to provoke him to anger.

"Therefore the Lord was very angry with Israel, and removed them out of his sight."

Had Israel remained true to God, wonderful blessings would have been theirs. They would have enjoyed great honor and riches. They would have been protected from the Assyrians and all their enemies. They would have been respected by all nations for their goodness and sincerity. Their cities and villages would have been models of order, beauty, and prosperity for all the world to copy.

But now, lashed by the whip of their conquerors, naked and barefoot, starving and frozen, they stumbled along the long hard trail to captivity.

What a mistake they had made! What a price they had to pay for turning away from God!

STORY 2

Youth With a Vision

A T THE very time that all these terrible things were happening to Israel, God raised up one of the greatest prophets who ever lived to speak words of warning and comfort to His people.

Just when Isaiah was born we are not told, but it must have been not very long after the death of Elisha. At least we know that he lived through the reigns of "Uzziah, Jotham, Ahaz, and Hezekiah, kings of Judah." This means that he also lived through the reigns of the last seven kings of Israel, from Jeroboam II to Hoshea.

If we remember this it will help us to understand many things that Isaiah wrote. How fitting were his words concerning Israel: "Ah sinful nation, a people laden with iniquity, a seed of evildoers, children that are corrupters: they have forsaken the Lord, they have provoked the Holy One of Israel unto anger, they are gone away backward. . . .

"Your country is desolate, your cities are burned with

147

fire; your land, strangers devour it in your presence, and it is desolate, as overthrown by strangers.

"And the daughter of Zion [Jerusalem] is left as a cottage in a vineyard, as a lodge in a garden of cucumbers, as a besieged city."

Isaiah's ministry began at the end of the reign of Uzziah, about thirty years before the people of Samaria were carried into captivity by the Assyrians.

He tells us about it himself.

"In the year that King Uzziah died," he says, "I saw also the Lord sitting upon a throne, high and lifted up, and his train filled the temple."

Above the throne he saw seraphim, each with six wings. Two wings covered the face and two the feet of each wonderful creature, while the other two were used for flight.

"And one cried unto another, and said, Holy, holy, holy, is the Lord of hosts: the whole earth is full of his glory."

The door posts trembled at the sound of the voice and the building was filled with smoke.

"Woe is me!" cried the young man. "For I am undone; because I am a man of unclean lips, and I dwell in the midst of a people of unclean lips: for mine eyes have seen the King, the Lord of hosts."

Suddenly one of the seraphim picked up "a live coal" from the altar of incense and flew with it to Isaiah. Lightly touching the young man's mouth with the burning ember he said, "Lo, this hath touched thy lips; and thine iniquity is taken away, and thy sin is purged."

149

Surrounded by the glory of heaven while worshiping in the Temple, Isaiah cried, "I am a man of unclean lips," and an angel touched his lips with a glowing coal off the altar.

Then through the smoke came another voice saying, "Whom shall I send, and who will go for us?"

It was the voice of God! The Lord Himself was calling him to service!

Humbly Isaiah answered, "Here am I; send me."

"Go," said God, giving him the message he was to tell the people.

And so it was that the prophet Isaiah began his lifework. "In the year that King Uzziah died," when everybody in Jerusalem was fearful and worried about the future, he saw the King Eternal, seated on the throne of the universe—the one throne that will never pass away.

This vision never left him. All through the reign of wicked King Ahaz, all through the terrible invasions of Israel and Judah by the kings of Assyria, he remembered what he had seen and heard that wonderful night. Others might lose heart, but not he. He knew for sure that God lives and reigns and must be victorious at last.

In the dark and evil times in which he lived he talked courage and hope. Someday God would raise up a Deliverer. Someday it would be said, "Unto us a child is born, unto us a son is given: and the government shall be upon his shoulder: and his name shall be called Wonderful, Counsellor, The mighty God, The everlasting Father, The Prince of Peace. Of the increase of his government and peace there shall be no end, upon the throne of David, and upon his kingdom, to order it, and to establish it with judgment and with justice from henceforth even for ever."

How comforting this promise must have sounded in those days of war, invasion, suffering, and death! Lest anyone should doubt whether it would ever come true, he added, "The zeal of the Lord of hosts will perform this."

Again he said to the worried and sorrowing people: "Lift up your eyes to the heavens, and look upon the earth beneath: for the heavens shall vanish away like smoke, and the earth shall wax old like a garment, and they that dwell therein shall die in like manner: but my salvation shall be for ever, and my righteousness shall not be abolished."

To cheer their hearts still more he said, "For the mountains shall depart, and the hills be removed; but my kindness shall not depart from thee, neither shall the covenant of my peace be removed, saith the Lord that hath mercy on thee."

"Seek ye the Lord while he may be found, call ye upon him while he is near," he urged. "Let the wicked forsake

151

his way, and the unrighteous man his thoughts: and let him return unto the Lord, and he will have mercy upon him; and to our God, for he will abundantly pardon."

At long last, he assured them, all evil will come to an end.

"Strengthen ye the weak hands, and confirm the feeble knees.

"Say to them that are of a fearful heart, Be strong, fear not: behold, your God will come with vengeance, even God with a recompence; He will come and save you.

"Then the eyes of the blind shall be opened, and the ears of the deaf shall be unstopped.

"Then shall the lame man leap as an hart, and the tongue of the dumb sing. . . .

"And the ransomed of the Lord shall return, and come to Zion with songs and everlasting joy upon their heads: they shall obtain joy and gladness, and sorrow and sighing shall flee away."

In God's good time there will be no more war, no more suffering, no more death. People will build houses and plant gardens without fear of invaders, and "long enjoy the work of their hands." Then there will be peace and friendship all over the world. "They shall not hurt nor destroy in all my holy mountain, saith the Lord."

Such was the beautiful message of Isaiah, the man who saw the Lord in his youth.

Isaiah described his vision of the beautiful new earth, free from all fear and unhappiness, where Jesus will dwell with those who have been faithful to Him and obedient to His law.

STORY 3

Angel to the Rescue

≈≈≈≈≈≈≈≈≈≈≈≈≈≈≈≈≈≈≈≈

TEN years after the Assyrians had captured Samaria they invaded Judah and tried to take Jerusalem.

Sennacherib was king of Assyria now, and he came up "against all the fenced cities of Judah, and took them."

Jerusalem alone was left. In all the country that God had given to the people whom He had brought out of Egypt, this was the only city that remained in their possession. All the others, from Dan to Beersheba, had been lost.

Never had the City of David seemed so lonesome, there on its mountaintop. Many must have wondered how it could possibly stand against all the might of Assyria. No doubt some said, "If Jerusalem is taken, what hope will remain that the promises to Abraham, Isaac, and Jacob will ever be fulfilled? How will the Seed of the woman ever bruise the serpent's head?"

Fortunately there were in Jerusalem at this time, behind its barricaded gates, two great men and one noble woman:

154

ANGEL TO THE RESCUE

Isaiah the prophet, Hezekiah the king, and Abijah, or "Abi," the king's mother.

Anxious to avoid an attack if possible, Hezekiah sent messengers to Sennacherib seeking to buy him off. The invader set a stiff price: three hundred talents of silver and thirty talents of gold.

Hezekiah tried to raise the money, even taking the gold overlay off the doors and pillars of the Temple. This he sent to Sennacherib. But the Assyrian king was not satisfied. He wanted more. He said he was going to take the city anyway and Hezekiah might as well open the gates and surrender.

But Hezekiah was not the sort of man to give up without a fight. He talked the matter over with his princes, and they decided to resist. First they blocked up all the sources of water outside the city. "Why should the kings of Assyria come," they said, "and find much water?"

Then they "built up all the wall that was broken, and raised it up to the towers" and made weapons and shields.

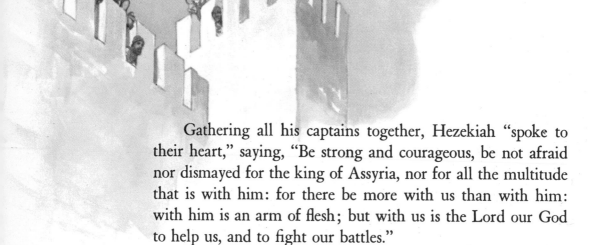

Gathering all his captains together, Hezekiah "spoke to their heart," saying, "Be strong and courageous, be not afraid nor dismayed for the king of Assyria, nor for all the multitude that is with him: for there be more with us than with him: with him is an arm of flesh; but with us is the Lord our God to help us, and to fight our battles."

Wonderful faith! Like Elisha, Hezekiah was sure the chariots of the Lord would come to his rescue.

The captains were cheered, and "leaned" upon the king's words, the Bible says.

They had need of courage, for soon part of the Assyrian army arrived, led by Rabshakeh, who called for a parley. Three men went out to talk with him—"Eliakim . . . , which was over the household, and Shebna the scribe, and Joah . . . the recorder." No doubt this is why we have such a full account of what took place.

ANGEL TO THE RESCUE

Rabshakeh told the three men to go back to King Hezekiah and tell him that there was no point in resisting any longer. If he was looking for help from the Egyptians, he was leaning on a broken reed. If he was trusting in the God of heaven, he was equally mistaken. Anyway, the Lord had told the king of Assyria to come and destroy Jerusalem.

At this Eliakim, Shebna, and Joah begged him to talk in Syrian, not Hebrew, so that the people listening on the city wall would not understand. Rabshakeh refused. Instead, he raised his voice and shouted, "Have any of the gods of the nations delivered their lands out of the hand of the king of Assyria? Where are the gods of Hamath and Arpad? Name the gods who have delivered their countries!"

There was no reply from the people on the walls, for King Hezekiah had passed the word to everybody, "Answer him not."

But when the parley was over and Rabshakeh had gone away, Hezekiah was much upset. He sent Eliakim, Shebna, and Joah to Isaiah that they might tell him all that had happened.

When they returned to the king they brought this message from the Lord: "Be not afraid. . . . I will send a blast upon him, and he shall hear a rumour, and shall return to his own land."

For a while nothing more happened. Then one day a letter arrived from the king of Assyria, repeating all that Rabshakeh had said and demanding again that the city be surrendered. When Hezekiah read it he "went up unto the house of the Lord, and spread it before the Lord." Then he prayed.

157

"O Lord God of Israel," he cried, "which dwellest between the cherubims, thou art the God, even thou alone, of all the kingdoms of the earth; thou hast made heaven and earth.

"Lord, bow down thine ear, and hear: open, Lord, thine eyes, and see: and hear the words of Sennacherib, which hath sent him to reproach the living God.

"Of a truth, Lord, the kings of Assyria have destroyed the nations and their lands, and have cast their gods into the fire: for they were no gods, but the work of men's hands, wood and stone: therefore have they destroyed them.

"Now, therefore, O Lord our God, I beseech thee, save thou us out of his hand, that all the kingdoms of the earth may know that thou art the Lord God, even thou only."

What a beautiful prayer, so earnest, so full of faith and trust! God heard it. Indeed, He sent Isaiah immediately to tell him so. "Don't worry," was the burden of the prophet's message. "Thus saith the Lord concerning the king of Assyria, He shall not come into this city, nor shoot an arrow there, nor

158

come before it with shield, nor cast a bank against it. By the way that he came, by the same shall he return, and shall not come into this city, saith the Lord.

"For I will defend this city, to save it, for mine own sake, and for my servant David's sake."

Wonderful promise! God Himself was going to defend the city. He knew exactly what was going to happen and how the enemy would be turned back. Everyone could relax.

That very night the angel of the Lord went into action. There was a great slaughter in the camp of the Assyrians. Exactly what happened the Bible does not say, but by morning light there were 185,000 dead soldiers lying all over the countryside around Jerusalem.

People crowded to the walls to see the amazing sight. They could hardly believe their eyes, for not an arrow had been shot or a stone thrown. Yet there were their enemies asleep in death! The Assyrian army was no more!

As for the mighty Sennacherib, "he returned with shame of face to his own land," where two of his sons put him to death.

STORY 4

The Sun Turns Back

ONE of the most wonderful events in history occurred in the reign of Hezekiah. The king had fallen sick, and Isaiah had told him that he was going to die.

But Hezekiah did not want to die. So he "turned his face to the wall, and prayed unto the Lord, saying, I beseech thee, O Lord, remember now how I have walked before thee in truth and with a perfect heart, and have done that which is good in thy sight." As he prayed, he wept "with a great weeping."

God heard his faithful servant. Before Isaiah had gone as far as the "middle court" of the king's house "the word of the Lord came to him, saying, Turn again, and tell Hezekiah the captain of my people, Thus saith the Lord, the God of David thy father, I have heard thy prayer, I have seen thy tears: behold, I will heal thee: on the third day thou shalt go up unto the house of the Lord. And I will add unto thy days fifteen years."

160

THE SUN TURNS BACK

How far it was from the king's bedroom to "the middle court," I don't know; but in the little time it took Isaiah to walk that distance the answer came.

Hezekiah then asked if he might have a sign that the Lord was really going to heal him.

Yes, said Isaiah, he could. And he could choose one of two. Pointing to a sundial in the garden outside the royal bedroom, he asked if the king would like the shadow to "go forward ten degrees, or go back ten degrees." In olden times, before clocks were invented, sundials were used to tell the time by means of a shadow cast by the sun.

Now, although Hezekiah was a very sick man who, but a few minutes before, had been weeping heartbrokenly at the

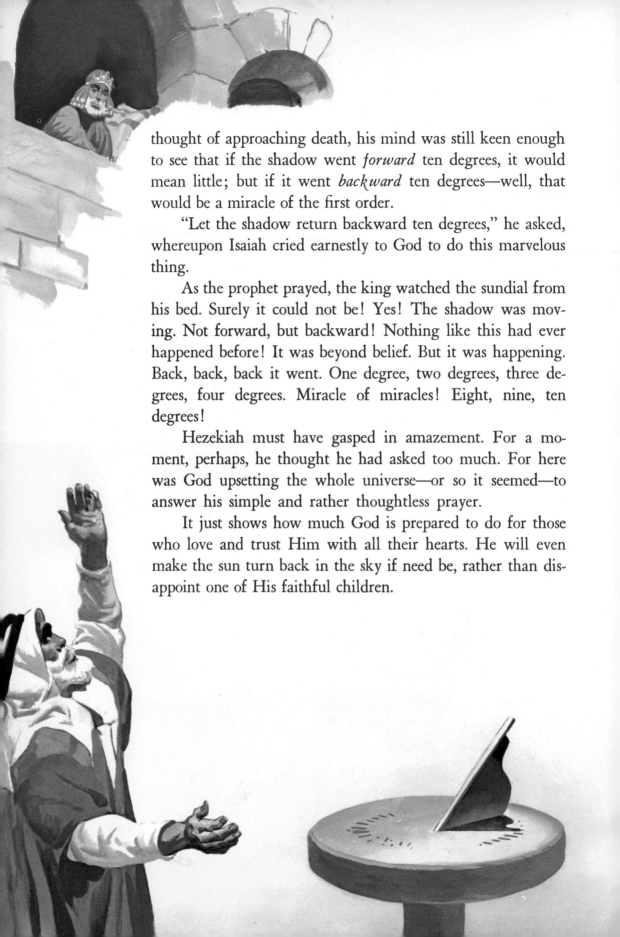

thought of approaching death, his mind was still keen enough to see that if the shadow went *forward* ten degrees, it would mean little; but if it went *backward* ten degrees—well, that would be a miracle of the first order.

"Let the shadow return backward ten degrees," he asked, whereupon Isaiah cried earnestly to God to do this marvelous thing.

As the prophet prayed, the king watched the sundial from his bed. Surely it could not be! Yes! The shadow was moving. Not forward, but backward! Nothing like this had ever happened before! It was beyond belief. But it was happening. Back, back, back it went. One degree, two degrees, three degrees, four degrees. Miracle of miracles! Eight, nine, ten degrees!

Hezekiah must have gasped in amazement. For a moment, perhaps, he thought he had asked too much. For here was God upsetting the whole universe—or so it seemed—to answer his simple and rather thoughtless prayer.

It just shows how much God is prepared to do for those who love and trust Him with all their hearts. He will even make the sun turn back in the sky if need be, rather than disappoint one of His faithful children.

STORY 5

Visitors From Babylon

HOW did the sundial miracle happen? Nobody knows. But it *must* have happened, for it was noticed at the selfsame time on the sundials in Babylon hundreds of miles away. And, of course, it must have been noticed on every other sundial around the world. Everywhere people wondered what it meant.

As for Hezekiah, he got better, just as Isaiah had said. Within three days he was back at work, as healthy as ever.

Then it was that he wrote these words:

"Behold, for peace I had great bitterness: but thou hast in love to my soul delivered it from the pit of corruption: for thou hast cast all my sins behind thy back.

"For the grave cannot praise thee, death can not celebrate thee: they that go down into the pit cannot hope for thy truth.

"The living, the living, he shall praise thee, as I do this day."

163

Some weeks later important visitors arrived in Jerusalem. They were ambassadors from Babylon, with letters and a present from King Merodach-baladan to congratulate Hezekiah on his recovery. They had also come "to inquire of the wonder that was done in the land," about which everybody was talking.

Hezekiah was delighted. Indeed, it must have been very comforting to him just then to find that he had a few friends left. With Jerusalem the only city in all Palestine standing out against the power of the Assyrians, he must sometimes have felt very, very lonesome.

So he gave the Babylonian ambassadors a great welcome. Gladly he told them how the shadow had moved back on his sundial, and how it had been a sign that he would recover from his illness and live another fifteen years.

Then with no little pride he showed them his secret vaults —"the house of his precious things, the silver, and the gold, and the spices, and the precious ointment, and all the house of his armour, and all that was found in his treasures."

What the ambassadors thought of it all, we are not told. No doubt they made a mental note of everything, in case it might come in handy sometime. They knew their royal master, the Babylonian king, would certainly be interested to learn where a nice little store of gold and silver could be found when needed.

At last the ambassadors took their leave, with many kind words and good wishes from Hezekiah and the people of Jerusalem.

Hardly had they disappeared down the hill, however, than Isaiah turned up at the royal palace. He wanted to know all about the visitors and what they had said.

"Oh," said Hezekiah, still very happy at what had happened, "they came from a far country, even from Babylon."

"What have they seen in thine house?" was the next question.

"Everything," said Hezekiah gaily, no doubt thinking Isaiah would be pleased with the courtesy he had shown his guests. But the prophet was not pleased.

Hezekiah had made a mistake. He should not have paraded his wealth before these strangers.

165

"Hear the word of the Lord of hosts," said Isaiah. "Behold, the days come, that all that is in thine house, and that which thy fathers have laid up in store until this day, shall be carried to Babylon: nothing shall be left, saith the Lord."

The king was shocked. He had never thought of this. Of course, he should have been more careful! Now it was too late. Those men had seen everything, and they would tell about it. His best-kept secrets would be known not only in Babylon, but maybe in Nineveh, too. How foolish he had been!

How careful we should be in every word and action! One thoughtless deed, prompted by pride or vainglory, can bring such unhappy consequences. Wise indeed are they who show their visitors, not the treasures of their homes, but the riches of God's love toward them.

STORY 6

The Bad Boy King

EXACTLY fifteen years after the sundial miracle, Hezekiah passed to his rest. Taking his place on the throne was his young son, Manasseh, one of the worst kings Judah ever had.

How such a good father came to have such a bad son is a mystery. It could be that Hezekiah loved the lad so much that he spoiled him. The Bible speaks of the "kindnesses" of Hezekiah, which suggests that he was a very tenderhearted, generous man. This may have led him to give Manasseh more than was good for him, and to spare him punishment when he did something wrong.

Whatever the cause, Manasseh was a little rebel from the start. He took delight in defying his father and going against his wishes. As soon as he came to the throne he set about undoing all the good his father had done. He gave orders for the rebuilding of the altars to the heathen gods that Hezekiah had destroyed. He brought back Baal worship to Jerusalem,

167

and "worshipped all the host of heaven, and served them."

His greatest sin was the placing of a carved image in the Temple itself—a shocking insult to the God of heaven, who had commanded His people, "Thou shalt not make unto thee any graven image, or any likeness of any thing that is in heaven above, or that is in the earth beneath, or that is in the water under the earth: thou shalt not bow down thyself to them, nor serve them."

Besides all this, Manasseh brought back all the wicked ways of the heathen. "He made his son pass through the fire, and . . . used enchantments, and dealt with familiar spirits and wizards: he wrought much wickedness in the sight of the Lord, to provoke him to anger."

Isaiah was dead by now, perhaps killed by Manasseh, who "shed innocent blood very much." But God sent other prophets to warn the young king what would happen to him if he continued in his evil course. Through one of them He said: "Because Manasseh king of Judah hath done these abominations, . . . behold, I am bringing such evil upon Jerusalem and Judah, that whosoever heareth of it, both his ears shall tingle. . . . I will wipe Jerusalem as a man wipeth a dish, wiping it, and turning it upside down."

But though God spoke so plainly to Manasseh and his people, they would not listen. As a result, sore punishment fell upon them. The Assyrians came and took Manasseh captive. The carved image he had put in the Temple did not save him, nor all the heathen gods he had worshiped. Bound with chains, he was carried to Babylon.

How long he remained in prison in a foreign land, we are not told; but while there he remembered his kind father and his father's God. He came to see what a dreadful mistake he had made, and he asked God to forgive him.

"When he was in affliction, he besought the Lord his God, and humbled himself greatly before the God of his fathers, and prayed unto him."

Very wonderfully, God forgave him—even though he *had* put a carved image in the Temple—"and brought him again to Jerusalem into his kingdom. Then Manasseh knew that the Lord he was God."

Converted at last, Manasseh tried to make up for all the wrong he had done in his youth. First of all, he took that ugly idol out of the house of the Lord. Then he broke down all the altars he had built in Jerusalem and "cast them out of the city." He also "repaired the altar of the Lord, and sacrificed thereon peace offerings and thank offerings, and commanded Judah to serve the Lord God."

So the bad boy king made good in the end. But what a pity he made such a mess of things at first! What wasted years! What needless suffering!

Manasseh's reign lasted fifty-five years. What a glorious reign it might have been had he always remained true to God and followed in his father's footsteps!

STORY 7

The Good Boy King

AFTER Manasseh died his son Amon came to the throne. But he only reigned two years. A bad lad, as his father had been, he was killed by his servants. Then his little boy Josiah became king.

Josiah was only eight years old at the time of his coronation, and that's very young to be a king.

He must have had a very good mother for, from the start, "he did that which was right in the sight of the Lord, . . . and declined neither to the right hand, nor to the left."

When he was sixteen, "while he was yet young," he gave his heart to God; and when he was twenty he began to clean things up in the city in a big way.

By his orders the altars of Baal were broken down "in his presence." He went personally to see that the idols were destroyed. As for the worst of the "sun-images," he cut them down himself. All the wooden idols he burned, scattering the ashes on the graves of those who had sacrificed to them. The

170

metal images were ground to dust also, even as Moses destroyed the golden calf in the wilderness.

Having cleaned out all the idols from Jerusalem, Josiah went "throughout all the land of Israel" and did the same in every city and village. Since the Assyrians had gone back to their homeland by now, there was nobody to stop him.

As he went on his way he asked for offerings to help repair the Temple, which had been badly damaged during the reign of Manasseh and his wicked son, Amon. Poor as the people were, they gave what they could.

This money was brought to Jerusalem and used to buy stone and lumber and to pay the workmen.

At this time an amazing discovery was made. As the money for the repair of the Temple was being poured out of the chest in which it was kept, Hilkiah the high priest spied a roll of parchment. Picking it up, he saw that it was "a book of the law of the Lord given by Moses." No doubt somebody had hidden it in this chest long ago to keep it safe from enemies.

Excitedly he called to Shaphan the scribe, "I have found the book of the law in the house of the Lord!"

THE GOOD BOY KING

Shaphan could hardly believe his ears. This was too good to be true. Everybody thought the books of Moses had been destroyed long since. Running to Hilkiah, he eagerly took the book from the high priest's trembling hands.

Yes! It was indeed the long-lost Temple copy of the sacred book written by Israel's greatest leader.

With the book clutched in his hands, Shaphan hurried to tell Josiah the wonderful news. Then he read long passages from it to him.

As Josiah listened he was deeply moved. Suddenly he realized how far the children of Israel had fallen into sin, how deeply they must have disappointed God.

You see, people did not have Bibles in their homes in those days. Almost the only sacred writings known, besides the Psalms of David and the Proverbs of Solomon, were the books of Moses; and not even the king had a copy of them. Knowledge of God's will depended largely on people's memories, and they weren't too good. That's why the discovery of this book was so very, very important.

You can imagine what Josiah thought as he heard the Ten Commandments read to him for the first time in his life:

"Thou shalt have no other gods before me.

"Thou shalt not make unto thee any graven image. . . .

"Thou shalt not take the name of the Lord thy God in vain. . . .

"Remember the sabbath day, to keep it holy. . . .

"Honour thy father and thy mother. . . .

173

← PAINTING BY MANNING DE V. LEE © 1955, BY REVIEW AND HERALD

When Shaphan the scribe read to King Josiah the counsels of God from the sacred scroll that had been lost so many years in the rubble of the Temple, the king was moved with grief.

"Thou shalt not kill.

"Thou shalt not commit adultery.

"Thou shalt not steal.

"Thou shalt not bear false witness. . . .

"Thou shalt not covet."

"We have broken them all!" the young king must have cried, as he thought of all the wicked things his people had been doing.

Then in silent awe he listened as Shaphan read:

"It shall come to pass, if thou wilt not hearken unto the voice of the Lord thy God, to observe to do all his commandments and his statutes which I command thee this day; that all these curses shall come upon thee, and overtake thee:

"Cursed shalt thou be in the city, and cursed shalt thou be in the field. . . .

"Cursed shalt thou be when thou comest in, and cursed shalt thou be when thou goest out.

"The Lord shall send upon thee cursing, vexation, and rebuke."

The king was shaken with dismay and grief.

"Go, enquire of the Lord for me," he said to Hilkiah and Shaphan. "For great is the wrath of the Lord that is poured out upon us, because our fathers have not kept the word of the Lord, to do after all that is written in this book."

Hilkiah and Shaphan went to Huldah the prophetess for counsel. She told them that Judah would indeed be punished for all the evil it had done, but this punishment would not come in the days of Josiah because he had humbled himself

before God and wept for the transgressions of his people.

When Josiah received this message he called everybody in Jerusalem and Judah to meet him in the Temple. When they arrived "he read in their ears all the words of the book of the covenant that was found in the house of the Lord."

Publicly he made his own promise to the Lord, "to keep his commandments, and his testimonies, and his statutes, with all his heart, and with all his soul."

Then he asked everyone to stand who would join him in this rededication to God.

While the people were repentant he told them of his plan to keep the Passover again, as of old. They were glad. "And there was no Passover like to that kept in Israel from the days of Samuel the prophet."

It was good that it was so, for that was the last Passover old Jerusalem and Solomon's Temple ever saw.

When good king Josiah died, Judah's last hope died with him. Little more than twenty years later both city and Temple were no more.

175

STORY 8

The Call of Jeremiah

AMONG those who wept at the death of King Josiah was Jeremiah, "the son of Hilkiah," perhaps the same Hilkiah who found the book of the law in the Temple treasure box.

Jeremiah and Josiah must have been about the same age, for it was when Josiah was twenty-one that Jeremiah was called by God to be a prophet. So these two young men grew up together, with the same hopes and ideals. They worked together in trying to clean out idol worship and bring the people back to God. No wonder Jeremiah cried when his good friend died.

As a boy Jeremiah never dreamed he would be a prophet when he grew up, nor did he want to be one. He loved the Lord and hoped to serve Him as a faithful priest, like his father. But to be a prophet like Elijah, Elisha, or Isaiah, oh, no! He didn't aspire to anything like that.

But God had His eye on this boy. He saw that he was

← PAINTING BY RUSSELL HARLAN   © 1955, BY REVIEW AND HERALD

Called by God to be a prophet, Jeremiah made the plea that he did not know how to speak, but God touched his lips and said, "Behold, I have put my words in thy mouth."

faithful in his duties; that he was a boy He could trust. And one day God spoke to him.

Such a surprise that was! For God said to him, "Before I formed thee . . . I knew thee; . . . and I ordained thee a prophet unto the nations." This was like saying, "I was thinking of you and planning for you before you were born."

Jeremiah found this hard to believe. He begged to be excused—just like Moses when God called him at the burning bush. "Ah, Lord God!" he said. "Behold, I cannot speak; for I am a child."

But the Lord would not let him off. Instead, He put His hand on Jeremiah's mouth and said, "Behold, I have put my words in thy mouth."

This was an even more wonderful experience than Isaiah's, when he was called. For while his lips were touched by "a live coal" from off the altar, Jeremiah's lips were touched by the finger of God.

Then God said to this rather bashful young man, "See, I have this day set thee over the nations and over the kingdoms, to root out, and to pull down, and to destroy, and to throw down, to build, and to plant."

Jeremiah didn't feel like pulling down or destroying anything. He preferred a more peaceful life. Anyway, he didn't like talking to people; crowds frightened him.

God understood. Patiently He said, "Be not afraid of their faces." There was no need for fear. "Behold," said the Lord, "I have made thee this day a defenced city, and an iron pillar, and brasen walls against the whole land, against the kings of

178

THE CALL OF JEREMIAH

Judah, against the princes thereof, against the priests thereof, and against the people of the land. And they shall fight against thee; but they shall not prevail against thee; for I am with thee, saith the Lord, to deliver thee."

Wonderful promise! Surely God could not have offered to do more for this young man whom He wanted in His service. He would take away all his fear, all his feelings of weakness, and make his sagging backbone like an iron pillar. He would make him like a city with brazen walls, which no enemy could break down. And through the darkest days God would be with him to deliver him.

Jeremiah accepted his call, and became one of the greatest prophets of all time.

Perhaps someday God will call you into His service. If so, remember His promises to Jeremiah. Let His fingers touch your lips. Let His words be your words. And don't be scared of people. "Be not afraid of their faces," for God will be with you, always, to deliver you.

STORY 9

Judah's Last Chance

TIME was running out for Judah and Jerusalem, but the people did not realize it. Nor did they care.

After Josiah's death everything went wrong. His sons were not a bit like him. They brought back idol worship again, and one trouble after another came upon them.

Hardly had Jehoahaz become king when Pharaoh Necho deposed him and put his brother Jehoiakim on the throne. At the same time Pharaoh demanded tribute of a hundred talents of silver and a talent of gold.

By taxing the people heavily Jehoiakim raised the tribute money, but scarcely had he paid off the Egyptians than the Babylonians arrived. They partly looted the Temple and took a number of princes captive, including Daniel and his friends.

During these dark and terrible days Jeremiah tried to bring to king and people God's last call to repentance. The depth of love in his messages is something to wonder at.

"Return, ye backsliding children," he earnestly pleaded

in the name of God, "and I will heal your backslidings."

"If thou wilt return, O Israel, saith the Lord, return unto me: and if thou wilt put away thine abominations out of my sight, then thou shalt not remove."

There was still a chance for them to avoid being carried away captive. They had but to repent.

"O Jerusalem," cried the prophet, "wash thine heart from wickedness, that thou mayest be saved."

If just one honest man could be found in the city, he said, all would be forgiven.

"Run ye to and fro through the streets of Jerusalem, and see now, and know, and seek in the broad places thereof, if ye can find . . . any that executeth judgment, that seeketh the truth; and I will pardon it."

"Amend your ways and your doings," he pleaded, "and I will cause you to dwell in this place . . . forever and ever."

How tenderly God spoke to these people who had turned their backs on Him and disobeyed Him times without number! How much He must have loved them to have offered them full pardon after they had been so wicked!

Did they listen? Did they care? Did they repent? No, indeed.

When God said to them, "Stand ye in the ways, and see, and ask for the old paths, where is the good way, and walk therein, and ye shall find rest for your souls," they answered, "We will not walk therein."

So long had the people followed their evil ways that they had come to like wrong better than right. "My people love to have it so," lamented the prophet. They didn't *want* to be good any more.

When the priests, rulers, and wealthy merchants laughed at him because of his simple, old-fashioned teachings, Jeremiah said to them: "Thus saith the Lord, Let not the wise man glory in his wisdom, neither let the mighty man glory in his might, let not the rich man glory in his riches: but let him that glorieth glory in this, that he understandeth and knoweth me, that I am the Lord which exercise lovingkindness, judgment, and righteousness, in the earth: for in these things I delight, saith the Lord."

As the days and months went by and nobody took any notice of him, Jeremiah's warnings became stronger and stronger.

"Lo," he cried, "I will bring a nation upon you from far, O house of Israel, saith the Lord: it is a mighty nation, it is

182

an ancient nation, a nation whose language thou knowest not. . . .

"And they shall eat up thine harvest, and thy bread . . . thy flocks and thine herds . . . thy vines and thy fig trees. . . . Like as ye have forsaken me, and served strange gods in your land, so shall ye serve strangers in a land that is not yours."

Again, he said, "Behold, I will bring evil upon them, which they shall not be able to escape." "Behold, I will punish them: the young men shall die by the sword; their sons and their daughters shall die by famine."

But nobody heeded his warnings. They called him a prophet of doom, and said he didn't know what he was talking about. Had not Jerusalem stood for hundreds of years? Would it not stand for hundreds more?

Sorrowfully Jeremiah answered them, "The stork in the heaven knoweth her appointed times; and the turtle [dove] and the crane and the swallow observe the time of their coming; but my people know not the judgment of the Lord."

Storks, turtle doves, cranes, swallows—and many other birds—all know their time to migrate, and obey it. But God's people, blinded by sin, couldn't see that the hour of His judgment had come.

STORY 10

Escape From a Dungeon

A S JEREMIAH continued to warn the people of coming judgment, it was not long before he got into trouble. After one sermon in which he had said that Jerusalem would become "desolate without an inhabitant" if it did not return to God, he was arrested and brought before the princes of the city.

"This man is worthy to die," said his accusers; "for he hath prophesied against this city, as ye have heard with your ears."

So angry were some of the priests and princes that they would have killed him there and then if a few strong friends had not spoken up for him. As it was, another prophet, Urijah, who had given exactly the same message, was put to death.

Another time when Jeremiah was preaching, Pashur, the high priest and chief officer in the Temple, beat him and put him in the stocks, where he was left all night.

ESCAPE FROM A DUNGEON

Next morning, when he was set free, Jeremiah told Pashur what was going to happen to him.

"Thus saith the Lord," he said, "I will give all Judah into the hand of the king of Babylon, and he shall carry them captive into Babylon, and shall slay them with the sword. . . . And thou, Pashur, and all that dwell in thine house shall go into captivity: and thou shalt come to Babylon, and there thou shalt die, and shalt be buried there, thou, and all thy friends, to whom thou hast prophesied lies."

With so many people opposing him or laughing at him, it was sometimes hard for Jeremiah to keep on with his work. "I am in derision daily," he murmured. "Everyone mocks me."

More than once he thought of giving up. "I will not make mention of him, nor speak any more in his name," he said. But he couldn't do it. The word of God was like a burning fire in his bones, and he couldn't keep quiet.

Thinking that if he wrote out all the messages God had

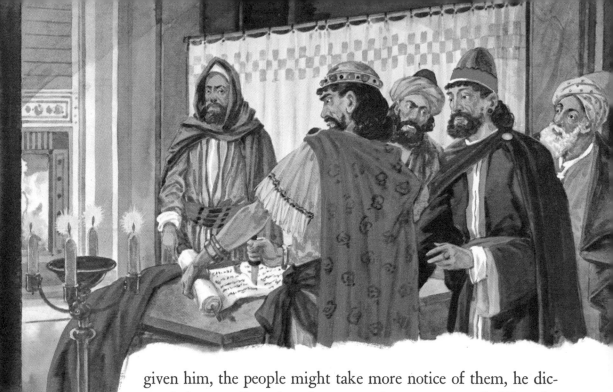

given him, the people might take more notice of them, he dictated them to Baruch, who wrote them on a scroll. Then he had Baruch go and read the scroll in the Temple. Some of the princes became interested, and asked Baruch to read it privately to them. But when King Jehoiakim heard about the scroll, he sent for it, cut it with his penknife, and threw the pieces in the fire.

After Zedekiah had come to the throne Jeremiah was accused of treason. He was caught leaving the city to go to the land of Benjamin, and the guard thought he was going to join the Babylonians.

"It is false," said Jeremiah. But they wouldn't listen to him. He was beaten and put in prison.

When King Zedekiah heard what had happened he sent for Jeremiah and asked him if there was any new word from God. Yes, said the prophet, there was: "Thou shalt be delivered into the hand of the king of Babylon."

186

ESCAPE FROM A DUNGEON

For this he was sent back to prison. But even so he kept on bearing his message: "This city shall surely be given into the hand of the king of Babylon."

Finally the princes could stand it no longer. They went to Zedekiah and said, "We beseech thee, let this man be put to death: for thus he weakeneth the hands of the men of war that remain in this city, . . . speaking such words unto them."

Zedekiah said they could do what they liked with him. So they "cast him into the dungeon . . . which was in the court of the prison." It must have been very deep, for they needed ropes to let him down. At the bottom it was wet and muddy and "Jeremiah sunk in the mire."

It was a terrible place for anybody to be imprisoned, let alone a man as old as Jeremiah must have been by now. How cold it was! How tiring, with no place to sit or lie down! How uncomfortable, with his feet squelching in the mud all the time! Every minute must have seemed an hour and every hour an eternity.

ESCAPE FROM A DUNGEON

Only one person in all Jerusalem cared, and that was Ebed-melech. He was not an Israelite but an Ethiopian, a servant in the king's court. He liked the old prophet and knew what a good man he was.

Bravely going to the king, he told him what a wrong thing had been done to Jeremiah. "He is like to die for hunger . . . where he is," he said. Then he asked permission to take the old man out of that awful pit.

Zedekiah agreed, and told Ebed-melech to take thirty men to help him.

How glad Jeremiah must have been to see the kind face of that dear colored man looking down from the top of the dungeon! I can almost hear him saying, "God bless you, son, for coming to my rescue."

Down came the rope. As Jeremiah reached for it he found there was a bundle of old rags tied to it, and a pair of worn-out shoes.

"Put the rags and the shoes under your arms," called Ebed-melech, "so the rope won't hurt you."

How very thoughtful of him!

Jeremiah did so, and the men began to pull. At last he reached the top, muddy, starving, and shivering with cold, but, oh, so glad to be out in the sunlight again!

What happened to Ebed-melech we are not told, but I am sure God must have blessed him for his kindness. As for Jeremiah, he was kept in the court of the prison, and stayed there "until the day that Jerusalem was taken."

189

Jeremiah blessed the kind Ethiopian who pulled him up out of the muddy dungeon where Zedekiah had thrown him for daring to tell him he would be overcome by Babylon.

STORY 11

Jerusalem Captured

EVERYTHING Jeremiah prophesied about Jerusalem came true. Just as he had said, the Babylonians took the city and destroyed it.

They came first, you remember, in the days of Jehoiakim and took away Daniel and his friends and some of the treasures in the Temple.

After Jehoiakim's death they came again during the three-month reign of his son Jehoiachin. This time they took the young king "and his mother, and his servants, and his princes" to Babylon, along with "all the treasures of the house of the Lord, and the treasures of the king's house"—just as Isaiah told Hezekiah it would happen someday. They also took away seven thousand soldiers and all the skilled craftsmen in the city.

It was then that Nebuchadnezzar, king of Babylon, put Zedekiah, Jehoiachin's uncle, on the throne, thinking he would be loyal to him. But he wasn't. After a few years he rebelled, and Nebuchadnezzar's armies came against him in great fury.

This time the siege of Jerusalem lasted two and a half years. As it went on, all the food in the city was eaten. "Famine prevailed in the city, and there was no bread."

At last the Babylonians broke through the walls. Seeing there was no hope of holding out any longer, "all the men of war fled by night," the king with them. They got as far as Jericho, but that was all. There the Babylonians caught up with them.

Zedekiah was taken before Nebuchadnezzar, who ordered that his sons be killed before his eyes. Then he was blinded, "bound . . . with fetters of brass, and carried . . . to Babylon."

Such was the miserable fate of the last of the kings of Judah. Little more than four hundred years had passed since David's coronation, with all the high hopes he had that day. Now his throne was no more, and, so far as anyone could see at the moment, his line had died out.

As for Jerusalem, Nebuchadnezzar sent his chief marshal to do a thorough job of destruction. "He burnt the house of the Lord, and the king's house, and all the houses of Jerusalem, and every great man's house." Then his soldiers went to work on the walls until they had broken them down completely.

Nothing was left of Solomon's beautiful Temple. The two great bronze pillars were broken in pieces, as were also

"the bases, and the brasen sea," all the metal being carried to Babylon.

Nobody was left in or near the city save a few very poor people. The rest were taken into captivity.

"So Judah was carried away out of their land."

How sad, how very, very sad! Surely the angels must have wept as they thought of all that God had done for the children of Israel since He brought them out of Egypt: the mighty miracles at the Red Sea and the Jordan, the glorious victories of Joshua, the wisdom and fame of Solomon. And now this! What failure! What disappointment! What heartbreak!

And what of the promises to Abraham, Isaac, and Jacob?

What of the promise to Adam and Eve in the Garden of Eden?

Was God's beautiful plan wrecked forever? Had He lost the battle with evil?

No. Dark though the night had become, a star of hope still glimmered. Faint though it was, it would grow brighter and brighter with the passing years.

God is never defeated. Far across the desert, in old Babylon, He had already started to build again.